In The End Is My Beginning

ROY CALLEY

© Roy Calley 2018

Roy Calley has asserted his rights under the Copyright, Design and Patents Act, 1988, to be identified as the author of this work.

First published in 2018 by Sharpe Books.

ISBN: 9781792191411

TABLE OF CONTENTS

Chapter One
Chapter Two
Chapter Three
Chapter Four
Chapter Five
Chapter Six
Chapter Seven
Chapter Eight
Chapter Nine
Chapter Ten
Chapter Eleven
Chapter Twelve

IN THE END
IS MY BEGINNING

ACKNOWLEDGEMENTS

Insert I would firstly like to thank my publishers for giving me the opportunity to write a fictional novel on my all-time heroine, Mary Stuart. Mary, or Marie as she is called in France where I live, has fascinated me ever since I was taken to the cinema as a 12-year-old by my older female cousin in the early 1970s to see the 'Mary, Queen of Scots' film starring Glenda Jackson and Vanessa Redgrave. Although the film wasn't a classic, it started for me an obsessional desire to know all about a woman who ruled Scotland – a place I have no connection to – and enjoyed the title of Queen of France, plus was the legitimate heir to the throne of England in a 16th century that was turbulent to say the least. This was a woman who can quite arguably be described as the most colourful and most controversial monarchs in the history of the country we now call the United Kingdom – a union that she desired in her life but was only achieved after her death.

As part of my passion for a lady who has stayed with me far longer than any real modern-day relationship, I have visited virtually every one of the castles, chateaux and palaces associated with her in Scotland, France and England, and was fortunate enough last year to be able write an historical and tourist guide called 'On The Trail Of Mary, Queen Of Scots', published by Amberley Publishing. I would even say that I have had a few personal 'connections' with Mary when I inhabited the space that she did all those years ago, two notably at Bolton Castle, but these are personal to me…and of course Mary!

I don't intend this novel to be regarded as the 'standard-bearer' of the story of Mary's life – there are far many better books available on such a thing and those of Jean Plaidy and Margaret George are especially outstanding – but I hope it gives the reader an insight into her mind and a desire to find out more. After all, that is what loving history is all about.

I can never hope to achieve the heights of talent of the aforementioned authors, but what I lack in that, I gain in the passion I have for the subject matter. I hope that is evident in the novel.

For those who are Mary-scholars, they will notice that I have taken some artistic-licence with certain events, such as introducing real characters into situations that they may not have experienced, or compacting moments for easier reading and understanding, but the story is based very strongly on the facts as they were reported and documented at the time. Introducing virtually every one of the players in the drama of Mary's life would need a book of at least five times this length!

Of course, the 'dream' scene with Elizabeth is a fantasy on my behalf (although it's entirely possible that Mary did dream about her beloved sister and nemesis), but I find it fascinating conjecture to think of such a meeting and how history may have changed as a result. As it was, the two were never to meet, but if Friedrich Schiller can write an extremely successful play in the eighteenth century on a non-existent rendezvous, then so can I.

Thank-you for reading and I hope you have enjoyed it, but my bigger wish is that you find out more about this incredible lady. Obviously, there is my book from last year that I would point you towards, but the history shelves in bookshops are overflowing with biographies and novels on both Mary Stuart and Elizabeth of England. A truly fascinating time in history.

Chapter One

My name is Mary, Mary Stuart, or Marie as it is called and pronounced in the fair land of France. It was the name my mother had too, but my father did not live long enough to know of such things. I am now a middle-aged woman who suffers from rheumatism and various other maladies that plague me, and I have been kept prisoner for crimes I did not commit for over twenty-years, yet I am a queen. I am the Queen of Scotland and I was once the Queen of France, and for my sins, I am the genuine heir to the throne of England. For these defects of birth, I have lived a life of misery and despair, and only now in my final hours in this cruel world, am I able to pray to God for forgiveness and to atone for the mistakes I have made, whilst at the same time hope for vengeance on those who have done me wrong. Below this cold and unforgiving room where I have spent the last few months, I can hear the scaffolding being erected for my execution. Even in my final moments, the gift of peace and tranquillity is taken from me. This time tomorrow, I will be no more. A queen will have been executed by a queen, something that should not be permitted, but I no longer have any say in my life. This time tomorrow I will have felt the cold steel against my neck and my life will have ended. I believe though that in my end, there will be a beginning.

I heard the door close and saw the light fade and at that moment I was alone, terribly alone. I felt lonelier than at any time in my life, and I am a person who has experienced the despair of frequent loneliness. No, maybe it wasn't loneliness, not that at all. I realised it was abandonment. It was the sense of complete betrayal, a sense of being completely dismissed, of no longer being worthy of people's attentions or thoughts. It was the beginning of the end.

It's midday, and the gloomy skies outside can't brighten the room. The window, which I've opened ever so slightly to help the odours of the morning meal blow away, offers just a single hazy beam of light that illuminates the writing desk but keeps the rest of the room in darkness. The one candle that I'm allowed is flickering at the far end of the room, casting ghostly shadows against the walls. They dance as if mocking my misery, taking on shapes of the ones who have been and gone in my life. There are so many.

This place, this chamber, like so many of the rooms and chambers that I have been held captive in, surrounds me like a cage surrounds a lion. I pace the floor as much as I can, despite the pain in my knees, and I breathe in the air that flows through the window, at times imagining I am in full flow on horseback in the ecstasy of the chase. In the evening I watch the sun go down beyond the wide river below and I prepare for the chill that the night brings. There is no fireplace here, for fear of arson on my part and so the dark hours are spent under the thin covers, sleeping in my bed. Each day has become the last and the next. There is no distinction, except that each day is one closer to the final act. My dear servants, those who are left and allowed to tend to me, scurry around and make sure I am fed and washed and exercised, like a household pet monkey, and they take the prie-Dieu with me, but I wonder at their faith and commitment now. My release will surely be their release too. I think that deep down they wish it to be soon, so as to unburden the shackles that tie them to this miserable existence.

I am still a queen. I have always been a queen and I have no right to be incarcerated in this way, yet my fight and resolve ended so long ago. How many years have I been at the pleasure of my cousin? Twenty-two? It seems like yesterday that I said goodbye to my dear mother country, not knowing then the lengths that Elizabeth would go to destroy my life, yet I am a queen. I am still a queen. I am the Queen of Scotland and I am the rightful heir to the crown of England and yet I no longer desire either. No queen should sit on a hard, wooden stool and look at the courtyard below and watch as her accusers laugh and make merry as they saddle their horses, ready to frequent the taverns and bawdy-houses before returning to pronounce judgement on me. I am a queen.

Like each place I have been imprisoned, this castle has gradually closed in on me, suffocating my life and replacing it with the fumes of death. Fotheringhay is a prison, a harsh and grey prison with damp walls and crumbling battlements, and when I was escorted on horseback through the thick gates at the foot of the hill, I remember turning back and taking one last look at the lush greenery of the countryside behind, knowing in my heart of hearts that I shall never see the like again. Never to breathe the clean fresh air or trail my fingers through the pure water of a loch or run barefoot through the meadows in the throes of youth and passion. These things are past. These people who have shared my life, my husbands, my dear friends, my family, my mother – they have all left me now, but I know they await in the next world, and I now feel eager to join them.

I didn't expect the visit, not at this time anyway. This room has been my prison for so long now, that I'd become used to the daily goings-on outside my small window to the world. I no longer needed to involve myself with other people's lives or cast judgement or take shame or feel sympathy. I just sat and watched and waited. I waited calmly and patiently, knowing that when the day came, I could accept and face it with courage, honour and gratitude. That's what I told myself, and that's what I truly believed. Now the day has come, and I feel like screaming, or I feel like crying, or I feel like begging, but I don't feel like praying. Not yet. That will come later. There is still time for that.

I close my eyes and relive the last few moments. Has this really happened? Now after all this time? Where was the mercy I hoped for? Where was the compassion? It was left to my dear friend, the earl, to tell me the news that I'd waited, and yes, longed for.

Shrewsbury was so nervous, so embarrassed that I felt exceedingly sorry for him. In the fourteen years that we have been in each other's company, I have never seen him so sad, so bereft. Has a jailor ever been so close to his captive?

"My dear Mary…" he'd said hesitatingly. The man who had been so strong and so forceful when we'd first met at Sheffield, who was the match for his over-burdening wife Bess and treated me like the queen that I was, now looked fearful and broken. His eyes were red and puffy and the black rings around them were results of little sleep. I noticed the thick grey beard hadn't been trimmed and his hair under his cap was unkempt. He was suffering. "My dear Mary..."

"It's alright," I interrupted and said softly to him, rising from my chair as slowly as my aching legs allowed. "I know why you're here, my friend." I reached gently for his forearm and placed my hand there. He looked down and I thought I heard an involuntary sob.

"Let me do this," snapped the man accompanying him and snatched the parchment from Shrewsbury's trembling hand. It was Robert Beale, a greedy man who I'd seen in the courtyards here in recent days. A young man with fine airs and graces, always whispering in another's ear of conspiracy and treason, yet never far away from the Royal Court when his duty and his naked ambition desired. This was a man who was known for his lack of loyalty to anyone or anything except himself; a man who hated my faith and in turn hated me. Oh, why could I not have been spared him at this time?

"Madam, I am the clerk of Her Majesty's Privy Council and in my hands, I have the warrant for your execution." The words were spoken with confidence and malice. He waved the parchment in a sweeping gesture towards my face, almost mocking me. "Please allow me to open it and read the contents to you." I nodded my assent and stared into his eyes. They were full of life. They blazed in triumph at me, his thick eyebrows twitching as he looked back at me, never flinching. This was a moment he would enjoy, and who knows how many times he would regale the impressionable with the story of how he gave the execution order to a living queen. That was for him though. I won't be disturbed by such nonsense in the future.

He had unrolled the parchment slowly, almost accusingly and for greater effect. It was as if he was playing to an audience, yet there were no others in the room save myself and Shrewsbury, who had taken a step backwards into the shadows of the candle. I could see his presence fading away from my life like memories of a dream that refuses to stay in the mind at the dawn of waking. Beale raised the parchment to his eyes and read slowly and loudly.

"*With all humbleness and solicit require to press the execution against her person...taking her into your charge, cause by your commandment execution to be done upon her person, as you think discretion allows.*"

There was more, much more, but my ears and my mind had closed, and I stood there, staring at the blank side of the execution order until he had finished, not hearing the words. When it was over, he rolled up the offending document - offensive to me but seemingly not many others in this cruel and barren land - and then resealed it and placed it into a velvet pouch that he'd been carrying. Only then did I truly see the cruelty this man was capable of through his eyes. They burned brightly and flashed brazen blue, his clean-shaven chin set firm with the thin lips barely concealing a smile, no a smirk. There was silence. "Pray ma'am, have you nought to say?"

"I have said all that is intended, but I would like to know of the hour that this will take place."

"Tomorrow morning at eight o'clock," replied Shrewsbury, stepping forward. "It will be immediately after the break-fast." His voice was unsteady, and I could sense that he was struggling to control himself. I smiled and sat back down on my chair, feeling the relief from the pain of the rheumatism that had become such a bane of my life.

"I suppose the morning meal cannot be disturbed," I'd said sarcastically. There was no response. "I have only twenty hours to prepare myself, for this time tomorrow I will be no more."

"My lady...," Shrewsbury bent down to face me, but I put my hand up to stop him.

"Please my dear old friend, do not despair. I have waited for this moment and I am ready. Death will be a blessing. Please go about your business and do not grieve too much, but I do ask one favour of you." Shrewsbury just nodded, and I saw the tears in his eyes. "Please fetch me my papers and account books. I have much to do." Shrewsbury lowered his head slightly. "Oh, and can you arrange for the restoration of my chaplain, Father de Preau please? I have not seen him for weeks, and he is needed to prepare me for my end."

"No, I cannot allow that," interrupted Beale. "Her Majesty would never be agreeable, but you will be supplied with a Protestant chaplain who will attend you."

"That does not please me. I will die as I was born, in the religion that I profess."

"As you wish." His eyes bore into me again. He had no respect for a queen, and certainly but none for me.

I turned to Shrewsbury and not wanting to add to his discomfort on this terrible day, I asked him one last thing. "Has my cousin agreed to my request that I be buried in France?" My voice was clear and strong, although I felt an inner tremble as I said the words.

"I do not know. If it pleases, I will enquire again." His was a mere whisper and he turned away quickly so that I shouldn't see his distress. Oh, how I will miss this man, if missing is possible in the after-life. Of all the men I have encountered in my life, he has shown me the compassion and kindness in my days of need. His burden has been great, not least in the ways of financing my captivity, but he has shouldered it with dignity. Whilst Bess was a happenstance friend, so quick to accuse when it profited her, he has been true to me. I can find no fault in him.

Before they both left the room though, a strange thing happened. Beale, who for the brief time he was in my presence had shown no mercy or compassion, suddenly stopped and turned around to face me. I had no idea what he wanted or what he was about to say, but what took place heartened my soul immeasurably. Without any prompting from myself or from Shrewsbury, he made the sign of the cross and left with the words "God be with you.", and then left. It stunned me as I never thought it possible. The earl though stood a little longer and I looked at his trembling face and felt such sadness for him.

"I'm sorry Mary..." and he too left. I was alone, and my fate was now sealed.

I am not alone for long, especially when Jane Kennedy, my dear loyal friend is at my side. She is weeping, and her crimson dress is crumpled with dark stains on the sleeves where her tears have fallen. She walks towards me and kneels, her watery eyes looking up at me. "My lady. I have just heard. This cannot be possible...this is not right...," and she sobs uncontrollably.

"Jane, my dear Jane," I say softly. "Don't fret yourself so. We knew this day would come. I prepared you for such an eventuality. I will die for my religion and nothing could make me happier." She turns her head up towards me. "Now come," I say reaching for her hand, "Let's sit and take stock. There is much to do, and oh so little time left," and with that I lead her to the table next to the window and we sit opposite each other. "I would like to say tis a fine day, but it's not" I laughed, and she smiles. "There, that's better my dear Jane. Please let me see you smile on this day. Now pour us both some wine."

Jane, who has stood by my side whilst all the others have left, loyal to the end, forsaking her own life for mine. What will become of her once I have gone? She is so sweet and lovely, but I fear is no longer in the fruits of her womanhood to be attractive to a suitor. How barren her life is, yet I still harbour a hope that Andrew Melville will be that person. They have spent such moments together, but her loyalty to me has tried and tested his patience, of that I am sure.

"My lady. I wish to swear allegiance to you for the rest of my days and keep your name burning brightly," she said as she swigged from her glass in a very unladylike manner. Dear Jane.

"You'll do no such thing! You will attend to my needs and then from the moment I depart this world, I release you from your bonds. You will live your life as merrily and happily as you can. That is my wish and as your queen I command it of you." Jane smiled again and wiped her tears on her sleeve once more, the crimson staining dark again. "Pour us some more wine, though I fear anymore beyond that might make my final day on this world a hazy one."

We drank and we talked like a queen and her lady-in-waiting can. We discussed how she would divide up my meagre belongings that have been left with me, and I promised her the rosary beads from around my neck. "No, my lady. It is too much…" she pleaded, but I would not desist.

"Jane, they will be a remembrance of me when I have gone. You will take them after my end and no-one shall deny you them. That is my promise to you." Jane smiled again and demurred her head downwards. We sat in silence for a while and I looked out of the window to the scene below. The courtyard was quiet, unlike when the lords were here in their finery and glory, eager to judge and quick to leave. Beyond the grey walls of the castle I could see a glimpse of the River Neal, its waters glinting in the pale sunshine of a cloudy day. The waves lapped at the shore as a trade ship passed slowly by, laden with goods so that the float-line was not visible above the water. I wondered idly as to its destination, and assumed the docks of London town, a near day away at least if the wind set fair. Oh, how I wish I could be free on a ship sailing to a new destination, yet those moments are far behind.

"What do you remember?" The question was asked without warning, and I quickly returned to the present. Jane's voice was quiet, and she looked into my eyes. "What do you remember of your life?"

I was taken aback by the question, as surely we remember everything of our lives, and yet it seemed a fair assumption that there may be perchance moments that I would surely forget. "I remember most. There are so many things…"

"Tell me one. Just one, if it pleases you my lady…"

I thought, and yes it would please me. There are few times in one's life when you can take stock, yet lord have I had the chance and not taken it. Now in my final hours, I could reflect on the moments when I could say I was truly happy. Not many but there were times when life was so wonderful and pleasing and there were no worries. "I remember Francois…" I said with a hint of a smile on my lips.

"Francois. The dauphin…?...but he was sick and died my lady, of that I know. How is it that you smile when you speak his name?"

"My dear friend Jane. In his sickness he lived every day as if it was to be the last. He laughed, and he cried, and he loved me as I surely loved him. I cannot be sad when I allow myself to be back in his arms." I rearranged my skirts and padded the pillow that was resting my back against the hard chair and began. "Francois…."

Chapter Two

"You'll never be ready in time!" It was Mary Fleming, one of the four Maries who travelled with their lady. She was busily tying the blue ribbon around the waist of her mistress, the only concession that had been made to the court tailor Balthazar who had been shocked at Marie's choice of white as a bride gown.

"White is the colour of mourning in France!" he had proclaimed in outrage. "You cannot wear that to your wedding. Surely blue or purple is a better colour to match the purity of your skin and your beautiful features?" He was scandalised by the whole episode, but Marie was about to become the second most powerful woman in the country, to add to her title as Queen of Scotland.

"I will wear white and you shall see to it...but as I do not wish to offend, I will allow you to design pretty ribbons and bows in the colour you desire." It was typical Marie, as she was now called in France. She was strong-willed and knew her own way, yet she never ever wanted to upset anyone. At the tender age of sixteen, she was wise in worldly matters, but naïve in the ways of the court.

"You look enchanting" said Mary Fleming, stepping back to admire her queen. "I have never seen a creature more beautiful. You will dazzle the whole of Paris."

"My dear Flem," replied Marie caressing her friend's cheek, "I do not know what I would do without you all. Even though I am to be married, remember that my heart will always be with each and every one of you."

Mary Fleming smiled and then moved closer to her mistress and whispered in her ear. "Are you prepared for your wedding night?" she asked mischievously.

"Flem! You affront me so!", replied Marie mockingly. "Anyway, Francois is far too fragile and weak to even consider such things, whatever those things are, as I am sure I do not know." They both looked at each other and then giggled before collapsing with laughter. Despite Marie being their queen and mistress, Mary Fleming, Mary Seton, Mary Livingstone and Mary Beaton all regarded her as a friend first and foremost and secrets and idle gossip could be shared amongst all of them without any risk of offence.

Their mood was changed instantly when walking into the chamber, unannounced as always, came Catherine de Medici, the Queen of France. Marie and Flem stopped giggling, and Flem curtsied half-heartedly and quickly left the room. Marie said nothing.

"You look radiant my dear," said Catherine rather acidly. "I do believe the colour of mourning quite suits you."

"Merci madame. I have been told it is a rather flamboyant gesture to be married in white here? In Scotland it is a tradition…"

"Ah Scotland!" Catherine interrupted quickly and waved her hand dismissively. "We will speak well enough of that place when it becomes necessary. You signed the document?" she added gravely.

"I did madame, although I do not pretend to understand its contents. I trust all is in order?"

"It is Marie. You do not need to understand any of it but pray be assured that you have done the correct thing." She smiled a thin smile and briefly Marie felt an involuntary shudder deep inside. The documents were presented to her only last week and she had no intention of signing them until she had read them all, but her uncle, the Cardinal, had assured her it was fine. Anyway, there were pages and pages of them, so how could she have read all of it?

"Now Marie, walk to me and let me re-arrange that pretty ribbon around your waist."

*

"The documents signed Scotland to France, didn't they?" asked Jane as she emptied her wine goblet.

"They did Jane," replied Mary struggling to remember what they said. Her memory was fading as the light outside with the onset of the February rain. "Uncle told me it was to safeguard Scotland due to the debt it owed France, but it was a trick. Just like all of it, I was tricked. I put Scotland under the protection of France and I didn't know it. I was…I am the Queen of Scotland and I signed away its rights. It is a shame to me, even now." A tear came to her eye, but just as quickly Mary wiped it away. "Anyway, I remember the wedding as if it was just yesterday."

*

It was the most glorious day Paris had seen in over two hundred years. The April weather stayed fair and thousands of peasants, paupers, citizens and traders lined the streets on the route to Notre Dame, waiting eagerly for a glimpse of France's most beautiful bride and the sickly young boy who would be heir to the throne. The entertainment had started nearly six hours earlier with processions and musicians, and street-jugglers and fortune-tellers, and all manner of food and drink. Fountains flowed with wine and every house along the route was opened for dances and singing, and whatever type of merriment took their fancy. At about ten-thirty in the morning the procession arrived with Swiss guards escorting the guests into the cathedral, all of them dressed in the finest costumes and jewellery. Musicians and minstrels from Scotland followed, playing their ear-splitting music, which forced many in the crowd to cover their ears until they had passed. They were followed by over one hundred men of the king's household, sumptuously dressed, ahead of the princes, abbots and bishops who took nearly twenty minutes to walk down the half-a-mile stretch towards the entrance of Notre Dame. All the while, lute-players played the melodies of France with young choir boys singing the hymns of the Roman Catholic faith.

Marie was some way behind Francois, who had entered the cathedral alongside his bearers and also his physician, but as she passed the crowd gasped. She was in radiant white. No-one had married in that colour, yet she looked magnificent.

"See how your people love you?" whispered the Duc de Guise, who was at her side. "You are the most beautiful woman in the kingdom. The people adore you, as indeed do I," and he held her arm firmly as he guided her along the procession.

Marie *was* beautiful. Her hair ran free down her back. Her head was covered with a crown of rubies and pearls, although not the crown of the dauphine as that was far too heavy, and her face was a mask of smiles and happiness. There was not another human being on God's earth who was happier than Marie Stuart at that time. The people delighted in her, yet secretly asked themselves how long a marriage of such could last, knowing the ails and travails that the dauphin suffered. His health had worsened, and even as he walked to the cathedral, some eagle-eyed spectators saw that he was being physically held up by the elbows on either side. Some had predicted that he would not live long, and Nostradamus had even suggested that his eighteenth year would be his last. More reason to savour the pleasures of the day then!

For Marie, this was a fairy-tale. In the final moments before entering the cathedral, she remembered the day she had been forced to say goodbye to her dear mother, Mary of Guise, and boarded the ship in Dumbarton on its way to France. She was fleeing the brutality of the English army who had continued their 'rough wooing' of Scotland long after the death of King Henry VIII, but she was just a child. She didn't understand, and her tears that she wept for her mother and Scotland had never really dried. Now here she was, about to marry the heir to the throne of France, Francois, her childhood companion, her playmate, her best friend, the one she had grown-up with in the extravagance of the French Court with its fineries and its elegance – so far removed from the barbarism of Scotland. Oh, how life can change…

If the wedding was spectacular, the reception was beyond even that description. For hours the dauphin and his new wife were entertained by processions, plays, dancers, singers and entertainers. At one stage the whole of the dining-hall of the Palais de Justice, which could hold at least a thousand people, was transformed into a sea-battle, with ships carried by lackeys vying for victory, as historic skirmishes were re-enacted for the couple. At the same time, two courtiers stood beside the dauphin and dauphine holding their crowns above their heads in a symbolic act of unity and union. It was only after around six hours of this gaiety that the dauphin announced that he had tired of the occasion and wished to take to his – their – bed. Truth be known, he was fatigued greatly, and his health was sore after such a day of activity.

*

"I wish I'd seen it my lady. It sounds so wonderful. You must have been truly happy." Jane looked across at me, her face lit with intrigue and excitement. "Tell me though. Tell me…" she leaned closer across the table, "about your wedding night?"

"Ha!!," I shouted suddenly. "He fell asleep!"

Chapter Three

Jane opened the door. I watched her as she less-than-gracefully pulled at the handle and it swung open. Standing there was the aide to the Earl of Shrewsbury. A sallow man who I know is run mercilessly by his employer and has arrived at the chamber panting and clearly out of breath. "The documents and papers that *your* queen requested." He said it with barely disguised contempt and I noticed that there was a distinct emphasis on the word 'your'.

"I thank-you sir. I bid you farewell." Jane's response showed him the politeness that had failed him, and with that she closed the door on the young man who was trying to snatch a glimpse of me, the imprisoned queen. Something he would be able to tell his drinking-friends in the tavern later. Jane came to me and placed the documents on the table. "My lady. Do you wish me to help you?"

I didn't reply. I was looking out of the window as the raindrops ran down the grimy pane, leaving streaks where the dust had been, lost in thought. Lost in my own world full of memories and dreams. "You know…I had to bare three deaths in under two years of our Lord after that wondrous day. Can you imagine?" I think the words stopped her as she stood still at the table.

"My lady…" Jane sat back down on the chair opposite and reached for my hand. It was warm and comforting, but I wondered if she could feel the bones of my fingers through the thinning flesh. Looking at her face, I wondered then what she could see. Did she realise how very old and fatigued I have become? Can she see that my eyes are dull, lacking in life and the once-full shape of my face is now withered? I know because I see it each time I look in the mirror, but how does she see me? My hair is no more, replaced by a wig that is talcumed and perfumed each morning, and even the fine and sensual mouth, the most prominent feature according to many, even that is now thin and turned down in sadness. There was beauty I am told, but a beauty of memory and not of the present.

"First King Henry, then my dear, dear mother and finally Francois." I can't stop as the memories are washing over me like waves on a shore. I look up and delve deeply into Jane's eyes. "How is a woman to keep herself with such a lack of fortitude? How could I cope?" but there is no answer. Jane stares at me in despair, and I lower my head and cry.

I don't know how long I cried, but I know Jane sat opposite me with such pain on her face, that I immediately felt guilty. I cannot put the guilt of my life on to her.

"Leave me be. I need to be alone," and I dismissively wave my hand in her direction. It is my command, despite the utter loneliness of my situation. Jane seems to understand, even if she is disquieted.

"I am sorry my lady. May I return at a later hour?"

It is said with such pleading and concern that I smile. "Yes Jane. Yes of course you may."

After she leaves, I am alone again. I close my eyes and I remember. I remember the wonderful days in the French court, Francois at my side, hawking through the forests of Blois and Fontainebleau. The long, sunny afternoons sitting in the gardens and listening to the stories of the Cardinal. The days of dashing between the rooms at Orleans with Francois, and me playing tig-tag whilst the Maries ran after us giggling. We were children, we were free and happy, but I know now that happiness is but a fleeting thing. It comes unannounced, stealing through the door to the soul and then leaves even quicker without a backward glance, and I suddenly remember that at the age of eighteen, when life was in the first flow and there was so much, so much to look forward to, I was widowed. I was motherless. I was bereft of the King who had loved me as his daughter from the first day he had seen me. I was abandoned. I was no longer the Queen of France and I was banished from the kingdom. How did life change so quickly?

I sit, and I listen with my eyes closed. I can hear the patter of the rain against the window-pane. I can see in my mind's eye the rider who has approached through the gates of the castle, slowly trotting his steed to a standstill and then dismounts. Is it a messenger for me? Is it a late reprieve from Elizabeth? I know not, but I cannot live for that hope anymore. I hear the muffled conversations outside, catching the occasional word but none that can add up to a sentence. It becomes quiet once more, but I keep my eyes closed and I remember again...

*

Francois didn't have to die. I'd cradled him in my arms whilst his uncaring mother, Catherine, argued with the physician. She refused the operation. She wouldn't let him touch Francois, yet all the time the pain in his ear was killing him. I watched him fade away and felt his body weaken and heard the shouts and accusations and all the time I wanted to scream – 'HELP HIM!' – but no help came. Francois was no more, and I remember the look on his mother's face as she bent down to look at her son. It wasn't concern. There was no anguish on that harsh face, but a smile, a glimmer of a smile. She'd got what she wanted. Her son was dead, and she was queen again. I can never forget, and it was at that moment that I learnt to hate as well as love.

*

There is a bang on the door. Insistent and important, yet I am alone here in my chamber so there are no servants to answer it. I wait for an announcement, but nothing comes and then the loud banging on the door once more. I prepare myself.

"Please enter but pray be aware that you enter the chambers of a queen who does not require any visitors." I said with my strongest voice, albeit I know I can hear it quiver slightly.

"My lady," and bowing deeply in front of me is Paulet, that most vile man and my keeper for the last few miserable years of my life. His presence abhors me, and I cannot imagine of any circumstance as to why he should be here now, unless it is one last act of wickedness. "I am deeply saddened by your predicament, yet it is not entirely unsurprising," and with that he stands erect and looks around at my bare chamber, a glint of amusement in his eyes.

"Please tell me what it is that you require."

"I require nothing my lady, except just one thing." He moves towards the bed and places his hat on it, before turning back to me and folds his arms. His affrontery is beyond belief and he sees the shock on my face. "Ah, the hat? It is of no consequence as the bed that holds you this evening will hold you no more after the morrow." He walks towards me. "I am here on a final errand from the purveyors of the true religion. I am here to help you turn your face away from the papist heresy that has bewitched you so and hope that in your final hours on this goodly earth, you will embrace the power of the faith of our Lord."

I sigh in resignation. Not this again. How many times must I have to endure this? I say nothing, but I clutch at my rosary beads and stare back at the man I have come to despise for so long.

Chapter Four

It is late afternoon and the food on my plate looks less and less appetising. Since my imprisonment here, my diet had reduced significantly. For the mid-afternoon meal, a few carrots, some hard potatoes and a sprig of basil accompany the leftovers of yesterday's pheasant. It's hardly sustenance, but at least the selection of sweetmeats bare muster with a sip of ale. I suppose there's little point in feeding the condemned.

I am weary. Weary from the news of this morning and the knowledge that I have so much to do in my final few hours, but just as weary from Paulet's visit and his non-stop haranguing of me and my faith. Can this man never let me be? Even now he is like a rabid dog that will not relent when faced with blood.

"You will repent madam. I will ensure that this will be as much as the day is long. The papist faith has no place here and I will not allow you to extol it, even at your execution."

"And who is it that gives you the right to refuse me the one thing you cannot touch, here deep in my soul?" I placed my hand on my heart, but his features did not change.

"Madam, my authority comes from the true queen herself. She has expressly forbidden you to take your faith to the block. We will not hear your Catholic ramblings in your final seconds. We will appoint a true Protestant minister to guide you to your end. There will be no rosary beads or such vain finery. It will be taken from you, of that you will be assured."

"Why do you despise me so?" I was weak, and I no longer had the will to stand up to this man. His hatred for me is intense, as it has always been.

"Madam...", his voice softened slightly as he took his place opposite me at the table, his cloak discarded on the floor without so much as a by-your-leave. There was no longer any ceremony he would abide by in my presence, "it is not you I despise, but it is your methods. I despise that from the moment you arrived in your barbaric kingdom you have attempted to promote your hateful faith to mine. Your reign is well-known madam as being the reign of a wild woman with your secret affairs, your lasciviousness, your delight in the sensual arts, your seduction of your secretary who paid for his compliance with his death, your murder of a truly-anointed king and the open and brazen way you married the man responsible not but a few weeks later. You are a harlot, a common whore and the world would be rid of you quicker than these words are etched on your memory."

"My Paulet, you are without reason and without knowledge!" I was angry and despite the pain in my knees, I stood up to face him, yet his features remained calm, whilst mine were a maelstrom of temper and frustration. "These conversations have taken place betwixt us too many times," I was shouting, "and yet I see that you are still not convinced of the real truth. My dear Riccio was murdered in a foolhardy attempt to overthrow my person, and in the face of a queen who was heavy with child. He was my dear servant and for you to continue to sully our relationship with your vile and disgusting suggestions, puts you in the light of the lords who committed the act. I beg your retraction again, but I fear I will not be satisfied!" I felt the tears rise, but no, I will not allow this man to make me cry again.

"Ah you talk of satisfaction, but pray, isn't that the thing you cherish the most?"

I composed myself. Becoming angry with a man who has a mind that cannot contemplate the reasonable. It is a fool's errand. "My Lord Darnley was a weak and unsure man. He pained our marriage with his coarse and unacceptable ways and was no father to his son. His death was of no surprise my lord, yet it is easily forgotten as to the number of plots he had endeavoured against my person. He was my love, but I have no guilt in saying that like the lily that fades away after the first bloom, so did my ardour for that man. I was not however, responsible for his death. Of that you may be assured."

Paulet stared at me. His face was serene and again I recall the times when he has looked that way in the past. The cold dining-hall in Sheffield where he ordered his servants to take down the royal dais from my chair, the chamber in Tutbury when he escorted me to the most hateful of accommodation and the trivial moment just last month when he dismantled the billiard table and took it away. It's a serenity of coldness and unconcern.

"And yet madam, despite your protestations, you married the man who was assuredly responsible for the murder of the said lord. Whatever morality that you may claim to have had, decorated by your papist faith, it surely left you at that moment. Is it of any surprise that your only true-born son refuses to acknowledge your presence, never mind your desperate claims of motherhood? Can a mother ever have failed so completely in her duties to her child? Is there any defence you could offer, even at this late hour, to somehow alleviate the reputation of the great Mary, Queen of the Scots? I fear not."

I had no answer. He was wrong of course. He was wrong in his accusation that I have failed my son, for my beloved boy is no longer aware of his mother or her fate, of that I am reliably informed. He was wrong about Riccio and Darnley and he was wrong about Bothwell, but these lies are becoming true in the eyes of the world. Is there no-one who stands by my cause anymore? I lowered my head as if in submission. Not as an admission of guilt, but more for practical reasons. I could not stand to have this man in my presence for one second longer. I have endured his hatred and ridicule and contempt for too many years. He has abused my nature and terrified my soul, and yet he was here in my final moments. I could not bear him anymore.

Almost as if he could reach into my thoughts and make them real, he stood and said, "I will not ask you one more time to renounce your faith, as I see that it is not a likely thing. You have carried your heresy with you the way you carry and clutch those beads around your person, but I will tell you now, you and your servants will not be permitted to show papist idolatry in your final moments. I assume you are clear on this?" He looked down at me and I closed my eyes to him once more. He walked to the door and then turned to face me. "I do not intend to find myself in hell after my death, but if I should perchance to be so unfortunate, I hope I will see you there as a permanent resident madam. It will be the only thing that would make my stay worthwhile," and he picked up his cape and hat, bowed courteously to me, and left. Only then did I allow myself the relief of tears.

Now here I am an hour later. My tears are dried, and I am ready to take up the work that I have to do before the morrow, but my thoughts are wandering, swaying like a branch in the breeze. I think of Henry Darnley, dear second husband. I quickly calculate that it is almost twenty years to the day that I last set eyes on him, yet the final image of his disease-ridden face is not the one I want to carry to the axe. I want to remember him when he was flush in youth, when he had the standing of a proud man, erect and tall, clean-shaven and oh how he could sing. My dear Darnley, with his enchanting smile and impeccable manners. What was it Elizabeth said of him? 'Yonder tall lad?' His kisses and caresses were as sweet as new wine, and he could play the lute as well as he could flourish the sword. In those first few months I could lie in his bed and never want to leave, forgetting the cares of the state and the demands of the court. He made me the happiest woman in the world when he married me, and there was nothing I wouldn't do for him. He took my innocence and my heart, and I loved him so, but yet…

*

"You are drunk again my lord." Mary looked down at the dishevelled figure of her husband as he lay sprawled on the bed, his shirt unbuttoned to his breeches and stained with red wine. On the table next to him lay two empty bottles and an overturned pitcher that oozed a yellow liquid. Whisky. The drink of the Scots, but one she couldn't abide, and yet many locals swore on its soothing amber as it reached their throats. For her it tasted like fire water.

Darnley had acquired a taste for it though. Too much of a taste.

Darnley looked up at the figure towering above him and slowly recognised his wife's form. She was again staring at him with contempt, that look that she reserved for him and him alone. "My dear cherished wife," he said sarcastically, attempting to raise himself off the bed, but his eyes were hazy and his head woozy. "I am glad you have entered my chamber; it's been such a long time since I've had the *pleasure.*" He struggled to right himself as he was tangled in the sheets, and after a moment or two of trying he collapsed into giggling, rolling on to his back like a puppy dog.

"Any pleasure you may believe you deserve was forfeited a long time ago. Look at you. You're supposed to be at my side at council, yet your absence is becoming such a regularity that it is no longer noticed." She continued to stare down at him, her face a mask of pity and barely supressed anger.

"Ahh the council. Yes of course my dear wife, my dear lady, my dear, dear queen, the council." Darnley somehow managed to pull himself up so that he was sitting on the bed, albeit unsteadily. "The very same council that I do not belong to. Am I right?"

"That is a senseless thing to say. You are the queen's husband and so you should be by my side in all things…"

"Aah!" Darnley put up a hand to stop her, "you say I should be by your side, yet you don't confer on me the one thing I desire, something that is fairer than your sweet flesh. You know what it is."

Mary knelt down so that her face was at his. "I cannot

give you the Crown Matrimonial until I can be assured that this union is to be as satisfactory to me now as it was when," she lowered her head, almost in shame, "we first met."

"You talk of me as if I am no longer alive. It is you who have changed your ardour towards me. Your love for me lasted no longer than the morning dew lasts in the warmth of a spring day. I see the way you look at me and I see the way you look at that man-child Riccio. He is your confidant now, and I am left to stew alone here in this prison that is my chamber. I am as much a king to you as you are a lover to me." He stood up and lifted Mary by her arms forcibly and put his face to hers. She could smell the drink and it revolted her. "I know what you are…"

"My lord," she replied, almost in panic. When he was drunk, he had a threat to his personality and she feared him in those times. "You do not know what you say. It is true that my love has receded in recent times, but you are wrong in your assumption over David. He is my trusted secretary and I need someone in whom I can confide in these troubled times. My love for you could be lit once more if I could see before me the man I swooned after all those years ago. If only…"

Darnley let go and turned to the table in silence, pouring out the last drops of whisky into the tumbler and downing them in one. He held the table with his other hand to steady himself, and then turned back to face Mary. There were tears in his eyes. "Could you?" He reached out and held her hands. "Could you find that love again my precious wife?" His voice was soft and gentle and almost pleading. "I don't know how I could cope without you by my side. I miss you so very much Mary," and he fell on her hands smothering them with kisses. He reached for her but taken aback she took a step back. "Please my Mary, come to me now…"

Mary stood firm and took his wandering hands in hers and stared into his eyes. "Henry, look at me" she said rather more forcibly than she expected. He stopped his attentions and looked at her face. It seemed harsh and unforgiving and not the beautiful and kind face that he'd kissed so many times. He stifled a sob, but the tears were running down his cheeks.

"We are with child. Do you understand? We are to have a child and he will be heir to the kingdom."

Darnley stood in shock. A child? A son maybe? An heir? He tried to take it in. There was no suggestion, no inkling, no hint from Mary. "Is it true? Are you pregnant? How long? When…?" All the questions that his befuddled mind could ask came flowing out as he looked down at Mary's stomach. Yes, he could see now, it was swollen ever so slightly. He hadn't noticed before, but then he hadn't been allowed to get close enough to his wife for so long. How would he have known? "Pray my dear Mary, please sit down and rest."

Mary shrugged off his concern. His attentiveness was not what she wanted anymore. This man who had fathered her child, her husband, was not the man she loved. She knew that she had to control the situation. "I do not need rest. My Maries have been tending to me, so I know what is required. You, however, have to be aware of the situation. This child is to be born as a future king and you will be its father, as indeed the act of union dictates, but you will be banished from court and from my side for as long as you are a prisoner to drink. For the duration of your 'recovery', the story will be that you have taken a malady, a pox of the blood, and you will require peace and quiet and solitude. For this time alone, you will absolve yourself from drunkenness and debauchery...and yes Henry I am all too fully aware of the stories that emanate from the taverns and the pleasure houses of the town in the evening," Darnley visibly blanched with the accusation but said nothing, "until you are such a man as to be the upstanding king and father to the heir as is expected of you. Do you understand?"

He did understand. He also understood that his nights of fun in the streets of Edinburgh had not been as secretive as he hoped. Damn the man who had betrayed him. He would find that person and slay him from head to toe with his sword and laugh in the process. He sat down quietly.

"When is it due?"

"The summer is the desired time. A mid-summer child is always a good omen, when the sun shines and the birds are sweetening the air with their songs."

Darnley made a mental note and yes, he remembered. It was probably one of the last times they had lain together. "You make me happy my Mary. Our son will be a healthy and brave and an upstanding child. He will rule the kingdom one day. It is an occasion for a toast is it not? Bring me more wine!" he shouted to his servant in the next chamber. "There is to be a celebration as I am to be a father!"

Mary stood shocked. Had he not listened to a single word she had said? Was this fool actually going to drink even more, despite her warnings? She ran her hand over her stomach, feeling the small bump and wondered what on earth the child would be born to. "I had hoped we could be reunited once this illness that affects your mind could be cured, but I fear I may be too trusting in hope. I bid you farewell my husband and I trust your pleasure in this news is treated with the respect that it surely deserves." She made to leave.

"Mary my dearly beloved. Please do not be angry anymore. I will change as you wish as I desire nothing more than to be in your loving embrace once more, and the cooing sounds of our child to soothe us both at the end of the day." He smiled at her, his teeth stained red from the wine, making her inwardly shudder. "For this final day though, please allow me to greet the news in the way I choose, as today I am the happiest man in the world, and tomorrow I will take heed and you will see a change."

Darnley didn't heed his wife's advice though. On that day he received at least two more bottles of wine and demanded from his servant that a new case of whisky be delivered. He wanted to celebrate the fact that Scotland would have a new royal child. At no stage, however, did this foolish man think of the consequences, or that if the child were a boy, then it would be a natural heir to the throne and Darnley would drop further down the order, especially if the Crown Matrimonial was not conferred on him. Instead he allowed his childish and boorish behaviour to manifest itself in many ways, insulting the lords at council, swiping a blow at his servant if his demands weren't carried out quickly enough and riding the chase daily, completely uninterested in the duties of court. He even allowed himself in his drunken and sallow moments to believe that Mary had lain with another. His mental calculation that had seemed so clear on the day he was told, now seemed hazy and he struggled to remember the times he had bedded his wife. As a seed grows in the ground, so the seed of betrayal grew in his mind until he convinced himself that the child was not his...but who's? There was only one person. Riccio.

Chapter Five

I opened my eyes with a start. Oh Henry. Oh foolish Henry. Such a boy and yet I allowed you to sweep me away in passion. What did you become?

It was time to deal with the correspondence. I've only around eighteen hours left, and already it's getting dark. The light is fading from outside, and the courtyard is now lit up with burning braziers that give heat on a cold evening and cast shadows across the floor and the walls of the castle. This is the last time I will ever see such a thing. The overwhelming sadness suddenly envelops me. Something as simple as gazing at the burning fires on a cold night I will be deprived of forevermore. The melancholy takes my mind. It stays with me for a moment and then I shake my head as a sign that I cannot linger on such things. Instead I pull the flickering candle closer so that I may see.

As well as the papers and documents that have been left for me, there is a box of my personal belongings. It's such a small case, no larger than a casket – ah, a casket. No larger than the casket that ultimately decided my final fate. The irony that it is the size of the weight of accusations against my being.

I turn the small brass key and unlock the wooden box and there in front of me are the only personal artefacts left to me. All the rich tapestries, the jewelled adornments, the elegant dresses, the trappings of wealth and royalty, even my cloth of state, have all been taken from me. What money I had been allowed to keep was stolen and now I am completely destitute, but what use is money when there is an axe ready to greet me in the morning? Everything, except my faith and the few articles of my religion, have now gone. I hold the rosary beads and whisper a quiet word of gratitude to my Lord that I have still got these.

I reach into the box and the first item that catches my eye is the studded pearl ring that I gave to Riccio as a token of my appreciation. It feels heavy in my thinning hands and the jewel has lost its lustre, so that it looks dull compared to the sparkle it once had. If there was ever an item that mirrors my life, then surely this is it. I put it on my finger on my right hand, and it lies there loosely, where once it fit like a glove. My bones ache just by holding it. It brings back so many memories of my dear Riccio. What a kind and loyal servant he was to me.

I recall the first day I'd set eyes on him, the curious Italian hunchback, no taller than a child, but he was dressed in fine array and his manners were impeccable. Oh and his voice! His beautiful melodic singing that was as sweet as a robin in the dawn of a day. I swear that I and my dear Maries all had to look away from him to hide the tears of joy in our eyes when he first sang for us. I played the strings, but I felt I was of no accompaniment to his wondrous sounds. He was my most trusted confidant, my faithful friend, my wisest advisor, yet he was the start of my downfall and he had little knowledge of such things. He advised me in the darkest hours and he soothed my fears when everything around me failed. The times we spent in my chamber playing dice or singing such melodic songs were of such happiness. I could spend an entire lifetime in his company, yet there were those who suggested deeds that I could not imagine. I could lay with him less than I may lay with a common peasant. It was his mind and his wit and his heart that I loved, and surely only Darnley could sour such a relationship with his poisonous thoughts and words…and eventually his deeds. Oh Riccio, my dear sweet David…

*

"Madam please save me!" David Riccio was cowering against the wall, clutching Mary's skirts as the assailants drew closer. He was screaming and crying, knowing that these were his last moments and he faced them with terror. "Madam, for the love of God, please call for help!!"

"I command you my lord to desist and explain yourself," shouted Mary angrily, still shocked by the sudden and violent intrusion into her private dining chambers. Mary Seton screamed as she saw the dagger glint in the moonlit room, and Bourgoing stood in shock, unable to move as he realised the horror of what was happening. 'I'm just a physician,' he thought. 'I don't belong here.'

"You do not command me my lady. You do not tell me, your king, what I will and will not do. I have seen enough of what is happening right under my nose, right under my bedroom. You and…" Lord Darnley stood there defiant at the head of the unruly group who had burst into the room, waving his sword towards the sobbing Riccio, "you and this…him!" His face was blood red, a mixture of anger but fuelled no doubt by more of the red wine that he drank endlessly, and he staggered slightly, but he wasn't the main danger. Mary knew she would be able to talk to him, calm him, soothe him and even offer herself to him, but no the danger was behind him. She saw Lord Ruthven, a visage as white as a ghost and eyes of hell, the Earl of Morton holding a length of rope and a glint of evil and Lord Lindsay who was shouting "Get the traitor. Hang the little Italian spy!" Running up the stairs were more men shouting and yelling after overcoming the royal guards and all intent on one thing. The death of Riccio.

"My lord, what has become of you? Why do you do this? You have been tricked by these people. I am not your enemy..." Mary was pleading, suddenly feeling the baby kick deeply in the pit of her stomach. 'I cannot let them harm my child. I cannot let them take me by force' she thought, but a dagger pressed against her stomach and at once she froze.

"Let us have the Italian blaggard and there will be no harm done to you or the child." In the fury of the moment she didn't recognise the voice or see the hand that held the dagger, but she was sure it wasn't Darnley. He had been pushed aside as the assailants advanced towards Riccio, kicking over the dining-table with its contents crashing to the floor, a jug of red wine seeping into the rushes like the spilling of blood.

Riccio screamed again and sank to his knees as one of the men grabbed his collar and dragged him past the sobbing and petrified Mary Fleming and the ashen queen. "David do not fear. Help will come," was all Mary could say as she felt his fingers being pried physically from the hem of her dress. She felt the point of the dagger pierce her clothing and the sharpness touched her skin. "My baby, my child!" she shouted in panic, but then she was pushed to the floor as Riccio was dragged by his hair out of the chamber to the shouts and cheers of the men. Riccio tried to hold onto anything that may stop it, at one stage overturning the birdcage that fell to the ground causing the chaffinches to fly agitatedly around the room as it split in two. He begged for mercy, pleading in Italian and French for his life; "*Justizia, justizia, Sauvez ma vie, Madame, sauvez ma vie,*" but there was no mercy to be found. Mary heard his screams as he was pushed down the small spiral staircase and then staring at Flem in complete shock she heard the final act. At that point Mary collapsed completely to the floor in tears.

Just below the stairs, in the main hall, Riccio lay with over sixty stab wounds to his body. The screaming had stopped and the cheering from the assailants was replaced by heavy panting and breathing after their exertions. One of them, the valet of Darnley, returned to the dining-room and looked at the scene of carnage. The queen was on her knees, being comforted by two of her lady servants, and the physician was in the corner, crouching and trying not to vomit. The birds were flying around inside, uncertain where to go, and the remains of the meal were scattered on the expensive rug that covered the corner of the room. He reached down and picked up the goblet and drank the last of the wine that hadn't been spilled. "Riccio is dead," he sneered, "On the orders of your king", and he left.

*

I open my eyes suddenly. I'm not sure if it's the sound of the rain hitting the window-pane with force or the remembrance of the moment I realised Riccio had been murdered. All those years ago, yet the images stay as clear and exact in my mind as if it were only the day before. I need a drink, so I reach for the flagon of wine and pour a generous measure. It eases my throat and calms my nerves.

Why should I have nerves on this my last day? Why are these images now returning to me, after they were buried deep in my consciousness for years? Am I atoning for my sins? Is this the work of God who is forcing me to relive my past before I make my final journey? If it is, then I am compliant. I know my decisions have been wild and at times impetuous, but they were made with the very best of intentions. Not just for my peace of mind, but for Scotland and for England and for James. Of this I can testify fully. I can also lift my face up to heaven and say rightfully that I have always defended the true faith, the true religion, and that is something that will never waver from me.

I allow myself to drift once more and the images return. Not of the body of poor Riccio, or of the love I felt for Darnley, but something far more sinister. Something I have closed my mind to for twenty years, yet here it is now, ready to haunt me. Ready to accuse me, yet I deserve no accusation. I did nothing wrong.

*

"My Lord God has given you and me a son, begotten by none but you...here I protest to God that I shall answer to him at the great day of judgement, that this is your son and no other man's son. I am desirous that all here, with ladies and others bear witness...but he is so much your own son, that I fear it will be the worse for him thereafter."

Mary looked at Darnley as she held aloft their new-born child. He gazed triumphantly at his queen with satisfaction, yet the fool had no knowledge of the true feelings she had within. Could he not understand by her final words what she meant? All the play-acting since that terrible night in Holyrood, all the promises of renewed relations between them both, all the tender kisses and caresses that she had to endure, the foul-smelling breath of the putrid man as he spoke and his pock-marked face of the diseased. Does he still not know that she cannot bear the thought of him? This, the man who put a dagger to the queen's stomach, of that she was now sure, the man who threatened the life of the child she holds now, yet he sits there and smiles. Mary will have her revenge.

"Please take the lad and bathe him," Mary says to Margaret Asteane, her wet nurse. "I need to rest." She beckons her to come close and whispers into her ear. "Don't let the Lord Darnley take him. I have ordered my guards not to allow him into the chamber, but you must be alert…"

Margaret looked at her lady with a pained expression, but she understood quickly. An imperceptible nod and then she took dear James away to be bathed, clothed and fed. Mary lay back fatigued and weary from the birth. 'Once I am strong again,' she thought, 'I will uncover the plots that Darnley has against my being. I will ensure that Scotland knows of the intrigue and treachery that their king has been plotting with my beloved half-brother to take the crown. I will raise an army and I will overcome their treason and my dear Darnley, the man I so loved once, but whose presence I now cannot stand, will be imprisoned for his wrong-doing. Once I am strong again…' and with that she closed her eyes and fell asleep.

Impending fatherhood had done little to temper the activities of Darnley, despite the shock of the night in Holyrood. He had never intended that Riccio be murdered, but he was overtaken by the forces of the men around him. They were strong, and he was weak; he had the good wits to understand, but he was also the king and they should acknowledge that. Thankfully his queen had immediately forgiven him and understood that he was seduced by the lords to do their work. She'd promised him that should the baby be born healthy and safe, then the matrimonial bed would be his again, and just as importantly, the Crown Matrimonial would be his too...at last. Ah, my dear Mary, can there be a more-sweet fair-maiden? He loved her more then than at any time, yet he still enjoyed the trappings of royalty.

Why should he give up the chase? Why should he give up the whoring? Why should he stop drinking? It was his right as a king and there was no-one to tell him otherwise. A kick to the stomach of the servant ensures his silence. A challenge of swords to the valet. A threat to the lords in the council chambers of their secret indulgence when dealing with the queen's correspondence. They were all but soft mud in his hands, to be crushed and moulded into whatever he may wish. No-one can touch him. Well nearly no-one...there was one who concerned him. One who scared him and one who would not be threatened or bribed or bullied. Bothwell. The Earl of Bothwell. He was the man who Darnley feared more than most.

Bothwell, that fine man, strong and full-hearted. A sensuous mouth that betrayed his cruelty and clothes that showed his Scottish gentlemanly manners, albeit they stood no comparison to the court of France from where he had returned. He was the laird of many clans in the lowlands of Scotland and he ruled his family name with a rod – and a sword – of steel and iron. He had come to the queen mother's aid, Mary of Guise, and Mary had called him to accompany her when she left France, so as to deter any English attack. The man was legendary. His legend seemed to follow him in the beds of his mistresses too. Now here he was, stood in front of him, his doublet made of gold-coloured silk and fluffed sleeves, satin inlets and lace ruff around his neck. The clothes were almost effeminate, yet they increased his masculinity.

*

As Mary slept, she dreamt of the morning she, Darnley and her courtiers fled from Holyrood. The dream wasn't clear or in particularly the correct order, but the one part that tipped it over the edge into a nightmare, was the one thing that happened. She relived it in her sleep over and over again.

"Darnley, you must slow down! I fear for the child within me!" Mary was screaming at her husband who was ahead of the horseback group as they fled through the mists of the early morning, traversing damp fields and wet forests. They were at a pace that was too fast, and she was struggling as she felt the child kick her hard. Her courtiers, and Mary Fleming, surrounded to slow her horse, fearing for her health and the health of the unborn child.

"Madam, we cannot keep this pace. I fear for the child's safety," pleaded Bourgoing, but they looked ahead and saw Darnley fleeing for his life.

"Darnley, please STOP!" shouted Mary as she brought her steed to a halt, panting and weary after the four-mile journey. They hadn't been followed so far, for what they can see, but Darnley paid no heed. He was terrified and was intent on putting as much space between himself and his accusers, the ones who had set him up to commit the deed.

Now they had turned against him and in their cowardice, had pointed the finger at him.

"Do not take care Madam. If we lose this bairn, we can nay say make another." He had shouted back, *"we can nay say make another...."*

"Shouldn't we ride a foal that is in spring....?"

In the dream they'd arrived at Dunbar Castle, yet it had taken on the appearance of Holyrood, and as she entered the gates and walked into the main hall, she saw that she was actually walking into the great dining-hall of the palace and there was Riccio's body, lying face down, his arms at strange angles, his body covered with blood. Darnley sat on a chair nearby, drinking from a jug of wine and already clearly inebriated, smirking and sneering at her.

"I could not wait..." he said mockingly, his face flushed with the rigours of the ride and the wine. "I am the king and my safety is paramount."

*

Even in her dream, Mary felt deeply ashamed of the man who once shared her bed and shared her love. He disgusted her, yet he was still her husband. He sat there, his hair plastered about his brow with sweat, with bloodshot eyes and leering at her. Another gulp of wine and then a crazed lunge as he tried to grab her by the waist. She stepped back instinctively and saw him tumble to the floor in his clumsy attempt to embrace her body.

"You are drunk again..." she said angrily.

"I am drunk with desire for my wife," he slurred and raised himself up on one knee, swilling the last of the drink that hadn't been spilt. "I demand I have what is my right my lady."

Mary stepped back once more and then saw the change in his face. From drunken lust, it quickly became white-faced fear. He was staring at something, or someone, behind her in complete terror.

"Darnley?" and she turned around to see Bothwell stood at the doorway, his huge bulk blocking out the light from outside, his cap firmly on his head in defiance of royal protocol, and the stance of arrogance and total self-confidence.

"My queen," Bothwell bowed in an almost mocking fashion and took a step towards her and the stricken Darnley. A whimper escaped Darnley's throat and it was at this time that Mary saw how truly frightened her husband was of this man.

"Is there anything I can do for you my lady…?"

"Is there anything I can do for you my lady…?"

"My lady…please awaken. It is Bothwell. Can I help you?"

Mary slowly opened her eyes as she came out of her deep sleep, feeling disorientated and unfamiliar with her surroundings. For a brief moment panic set in, but quickly her eyes adjusted to the scene around her, and she saw the Earl of Bothwell looking down at her, tenderly and with compassion.

"I am glad you awake my lady" as he stood back and looked around him. "I believe that your husband has left your side once more?" The accusation was clear, and it was distasteful to him. "Young Fleming had the presence of her wits to call for me when it was clear that you lay here with naught around you, except the young bairn next door, and I believe that he will be of little use at this time. I am here to serve my queen," and he gave an extravagant bow, sweeping his hat before him and smiling at Mary.

For the first time since the terrible night of Riccio's murder, she felt safe and comforted. This man, brute that he was, took no arguing and few men would attempt to single-handedly. This man, who was of such a presence with her dear mother, was now here, standing at her side and ready to protect her from whatever evils the world had in store.

Chapter Six

Ah Bothwell...I open my eyes and the light has faded even more. There is a chill in the air and I wrap my shawl around my shoulders tighter, but I can still see the small vapours of my breath each time I breathe. There is little point in asking the guards to light the fire again, as they will surely refuse me once more, even on this my final night. On the table in front of me is the small casket, still open. I push the ring to one side, shuddering at the memories it has brought back, and then pull out the folded letter. It feels so familiar in my hand, and even before opening it once more, I know exactly its contents. It is the letter that he gave to me at Carberry Hill before he left. I have treasured it ever since that fateful day, sometimes reading and rereading as I sat in my captivity. Whatever became of Bothwell? Where did he go?

I don't realise, but Mary Seton has entered the room and is stood by me. My dear Seton, the loyalist of all my Maries, the one who didn't leave for the love of a man but kept her love for me bright and shining in the moments of darkness, and this is now surely the blackest.

"It's Bothwell's letter?" she asks, although she has seen it many times.

I smile in acknowledgement and she sits down opposite me. I can tell that she has been crying heavily, but she has tried to cover up the streaks of tears with powder. Her eyes are still puffy, and I reach out and touch her hand. "Ne pleure pas pour moi."

We sit in the gloom and I read out the letter again, not that either of us have forgotten a single word of its contents. It heartened me then and it heartens me now.

'*My loving Mary. know that, although we be parted, I will always be at your side. No foreign armies of any divers sort can separate us and even though I leave you now in the trust of the lords, I shall return, and we will together defeat these men and their blaggards and rule this kingdom together. You are the one true love I desire and the one true love I have found. Whether you be queen or scullery-maid, my love would remain the same. Do not fear. Stay strong and I will return on the morrow with a thousand fighting soldiers to your cause. My loving Mary. your loving James.*'

"I never saw him again," I say wistfully as I fold up the letter for probably the last time in my life. "Some say he perished at sea, yet others say he was captured in Denmark and was left mad of the flux of the mind in the dungeon of his prison. Whatever, he did not return..."

"You didn't love him though my lady..."

It was said unexpectedly, and I was taken aback briefly, but deep down I knew it was true. I didn't love Bothwell, but I relied on him. Oh my, how I relied on that strong man. The one who could protect me and save the kingdom, yet he left when his presence was needed so badly.

"You are right Seton, but he was a good man." I saw her raise her eyebrows in a questioning way and I rebuke her sharply. "Whatever you or others may think, he never did me any wrong, unlike so many..."

"That may be so my lady, but he was responsible for your plight. T'was the reason why you fled. T'was the reason why you are imprisoned. Oh, for not the chance of meeting that man again and you could put so many wrongs right."

"You talk of Darnley…?" I ask irritably.

"Yes Mary." Seton hardly calls me by my name now. I have become 'my lady' ever since I was made Queen of France, yet there is something soothing about hearing her call me Mary the way she used to when we were children. I smile.

"Are you going to rebuke me the way you did when the games we played as children became too unruly? Is that your aim now?"

Seton has a grin on her face and it lights up the room, but then it fades, and she becomes serious and stern. She leans towards me and whispers. "Did he ever tell you what happened? Did he ever admit to the act? You never speak of that night, yet his guilt is clear to all except those who are close. Has he ever told the story?"

I know what she refers to, and it's true that for years I have never spoken of the evening. It is for me, a moment that I hope to smother so that it never sees the light of life again, yet it will always follow me, even in my death. Darnley's murder.

*

"I do not want to stay in the provost's house. I want to stay with you." Darnley was complaining like an errant child as the litter he was being carried in bounced and bumped over the stone road. He was alone with Mary, his face covered by a taffeta to hide the appalling blemishes caused by the sickness. His vanity was such that he could not bear anyone to see him that way. Mary sat opposite, listening to this pathetic man whine and moan like a kitten, wincing visibly every time he opened his mouth as the foul odour of his breath filled up the space between them. She raised a handkerchief to her face and replied quietly.

"It is far safer for you there than any other lodging. You have enemies all around you. This is prudent and wise, and besides," she forced a smile and took away the perfumed cloth from her nose, "it means we can be closer together."

That cheered Darnley immensely. In fact, he hadn't been happier for such a long time, and that was because his dear Mary had somehow softened towards him, even bringing him to Edinburgh so that he could rid himself of the cursed pox that travailed his body. Once he was clean, she had promised he could return to her bed and they could renew their marriage duties. It was what kept him happy in the dark days of the pain and discomfort of his illness. 'Oh, to find the whore who gave me this ailment. I would perchance find her and slit her stomach and watch as the gullet spills its contents' he thought angrily. His mind raced as he attempted to place the one who must have given him the disease, but there had been so many. Each one was willing, and each one played the role of the queen, yet each one dirtier than the last. He'd had his fill of foul-smelling, pox-ridden whores who charged the more once they hinted that it was the king who came calling. They should service me for free, yet they all wanted a pound of flesh for his manhood. 'Ahh, but such sweet moments...' They were over now, because Mary had relented and taken him back. She was here in the litter with him, and she was taking him to Edinburgh to help him recover. What more could a wife do for her loving husband?

Mary sat there and tried to disguise her loathing for the creature sat opposite her. She desperately didn't want to be anywhere near the disgusting and vile man, but the moment she'd learnt of the plots that Darnley had been accused of, she had only one option; bring him back to Edinburgh and keep him close, until she knew what to do with her husband.

It was Bothwell who had warned her of the impending danger to her and her son. The danger came from Darnley. He had plotted with King Phillip of Spain to overthrow Mary and take the crown for himself. Well that is what he believed. He'd sent letters to Spain telling them that the true Catholic cause was being tested in Scotland because Mary had Protestant friends, and so surely having Darnley as the one and only King of Scotland would ensure that Catholicism would endure in the country? Phillip had replied in a non-descript manner, suggesting that he would support Darnley in his quest for the crown, but offering nothing in the way of assistance. It was a typically foolish and childish scheme that only Darnley could take seriously, but it was sufficient for Bothwell and Mary's courtiers to be concerned. Of course, Darnley denied all knowledge of such a conspiracy.

"I do not know what you refer to my lord!", he'd cried out in anguish and guilt, his face reddening as he realised he had been duped again, and very quickly. "It wasn't me who plotted…it was them…I was not involved…in fact, I was going to come and tell you and my dear lady, but you arrived in such a time that I had no opportunity. I swear to you on the life of all those I hold dear, that I did not have any knowledge of these plots at all." He stood facing the lords, Bothwell included, and he felt himself tremble. He put his hands behind his back so that they could not see them shake, and he so wished at that time that he had a flagon of wine to soothe his dry throat. It was Bothwell who spoke.

"It is clear that you need to be taken away from this place. You have a sickness of the body as well as of the mind and there can not be any more stories of the king fraternising with the harlots. There are too many wild rumours of your drinking and base behaviour..." Darnley puffed his chest out and was about to explode in anger, but Bothwell put up a hand which was enough to stop him. "And due to the illness that the king has contracted, then the queen has requested that you return to Edinburgh where you will be...taken care of."

"The queen...?" stammered Darnley. "She has requested?"

"Yes my lord," replied Bothwell with little relish. "She will join you on the journey. She wants to make sure you arrive safely and in one piece. She fears for your safety after hearing of the plots that have been attributed to you. She believes that there may be many who wish to do the king harm, and that is something that cannot be allowed."

Darnley suddenly felt a rush of relief and joy at the news that Mary was personally escorting him back to the palace in Edinburgh. That relief stayed with him throughout the long and tedious journey, especially as his beloved wife was sat opposite him. He had no idea that each time he drew a breath and exhaled, the stench made Mary feel quite sick, despite the handkerchief she kept to her nose that had to be dipped into the lavender perfume bottle. He also had no idea that the taffeta that covered his face was of a relief to Mary, so she did not have to look at him. For him the pleasure was the company of his wife and the promise of treats to come. Like the business with Riccio, the plots that he had been involved with can be forgotten quickly once the two of them were reunited. For Mary, it was another problem to deal with. The lord of Moray, her half-brother, and his Protestant gatherings were rebelling, urged on by the odious John Knox. Not only did she have to deal with the firebrand in the pulpit screaming his words of fire and hatred towards her, but her very brother had turned his back on her and now threatened her removal from the crown by force. Darnley was of little consequence through all of this, but he was like a moth attracted to a flame, and the only way to get rid of the irritation was not by extinguishing the flame, but by dealing with the moth…but how?

It was three days later, three nights of the constant whimpering of Darnley as he begged and pleaded for Mary to stay with him in his chamber for one evening, but the queen had no mind to. She was completely unsure as to what to do about her husband. She no longer loved him, and actually felt disgust at his presence, but she didn't wish any harm even though the plotting with Spain had been easily discovered. Even Knox, in one of his many visits, had taken time out from his lambasting and preaching at her to admit that the king's actions were of a 'stupid little boy who barely resembles that of a man.' There seemed little but to keep him close at hand, something which was easy in his current condition, but also caused her and Darnley's servants dismay at having to deal with the rotting body that he had become. Even regular baths in mercury had made little or no difference. The truth was, Darnley was dying.

Soon she wouldn't need to be burdened by his presence. It was harsh, but sadly that was how he had become to her, all of his own making. How could she have loved him all those years ago?

"I must return to the palace for the festivities. I have agreed to be the maid-of-honour, and a queen cannot let her subjects down." Mary sat near the bed, as close as she could without feeling nauseas. Darnley lay propped up on a feather pillow, the taffeta still across his face as the sores had started to ooze. His breath was still putrid, but he'd been advised to rub his teeth and gums with the bark of an acorn tree but had made little difference. He was aware of her distaste for him as it was clear in his sorrowful eyes, and for a few moments Mary felt saddened. This was the man she had fallen passionately in love with and had desired more than any other. They had a child together, and yet he had become another entirely. "Henry…" she placed her hands on the bedcover, the closest she could without touching him, "how did this happen? How have we become as two when we were once just one?"

For a moment there was silence. Darnley had noticed she had called him by his first name, and that made his heart jump, but the question was one of finality. He could have at that time then showed compassion and humility. He could have shown love and understanding. He could have reached out as a husband reaches out to his wife, but he didn't. "You wouldn't give me the Crown Matrimonial…" he stated in a hurt and childish tone. "You promised, and you didn't give it to me…"

Mary shook her head, stood up and turned around, dazed by his stupidity once again. As she got to the door, she stopped and looked back at her husband. "For what did I deserve you? I state now that it is of no more interest to me what your intentions are. I am weary and tired of your behaviour. You could never wear the crown and I will never give it to you. Farewell my long, lost husband" and she left, never to see Darnley again.

As she descended the spiral staircase that led to the ground floor, she could hear the muffled movements of people in the cellar below. It sounded like heavy boxes and sacks were being dragged across the floor. She turned to Lady Reres, her companion, and remarked on it.

"At this hour? It is noise enough to keep the dead awake, nought mind waking them in the first place." The Lady smiled back at her and they continued to the bottom of the stairs where they were confronted by Paris, Bothwell's loyal servant. His face was black.

"Paris, how begrimed you are," said Mary and she passed by him to her horse and litter. Lady Reres gave a conspiratorial nod to Paris and continued. He watched as the queen and her lady disappeared up the hill back to the palace in the fading moonlight, and then returned to his task. It had taken most of the day, and there were still at least twelve more sacks to be hauled up the pathway into the cellar. 'The devil's work…' he thought.

Darnley lay in his bed, sulking as usual. The room was now empty, save for him and his servant Nelson. The candles cast dancing shadows against the walls, and Darnley felt uncomfortable, and truth be known, scared too. He was aware of the distaste at which he was held by the lords, and the very same who had involved him in the murder of Riccio, had now turned against him after his cowardly fleeing from Holyrood Palace. There were rumours of plots against him as the Lords Morton and Moray were now convinced that only his death could end all association with that bloody night. Also, his plotting against the queen was now common knowledge amongst the royal courtiers, even though in his own mind, he was convinced that Mary had forgiven him and was ready to reconcile the two of them. That was of course, until that evening.

"I hear noises Nelson. This house feels haunted. Do you hear the sounds?"

Nelson rose from his bed at the foot of Darnley's and listened intently. "I believe it's just the wind my lord. This is an old house, so the groans are perchance that of the wood that has seen a better time."

"It cannot be the wind surely? There are footsteps below, of that I am sure."

"My lord, I have heard nought of such things, yet the creaking of the floorboards is all that can be heard."

Darnley wasn't convinced though, and he walked to the window and looked down at the street below. Kirk o'Field was a dismal place to lodge the king. It was old and dirty and outside the safety of the city walls, even though his chamber had been dressed with the best tapestries from his room in the palace, and his bed was covered in red velvet, it felt unclean, unsafe and vulnerable. Outside his room there was no-one. No guards and no servants to do his bidding. No protection should he be assailed during the night. It was not a kingly lodging at all, no matter what Mary had promised. He was here alone with Nelson, and what good would he be in an attack? He felt sullen and miserable, especially after she had walked out in anger earlier that evening. How can he understand this woman? She promises so much and then just as quickly she takes it away. 'I despair of ever making her happy,' he thought, 'yet she is the one I love. She is the one I desire, but I fear there may now be another. Oh, pray it is not that man-brute Bothwell. Please do not submit to his wiles and deceits.'

Suddenly a louder noise disturbed them both. It sounded like footsteps on the staircase. Darnley froze in fear and stared at Nelson. The room suddenly felt very cold as if a door had been blown open and the night chill had entered. "We have to flee!" whispered Darnley, and he opened the window which was set stuck against the rotten wood of the pane.

"Your shawl my lord..." said Nelson, looking for the discarded clothing that Darnley had thrown to the floor when getting into bed.

"There is no time," cried Darnley in an agitated state, and he somehow managed to wrench the window free from the wood, breaking the pane in the process. "I would rather die of the cold than face what is behind that door." His voice was trembling. He climbed through the window, dressed in only his nightgown, and jumped the ten feet or so to the ground, twisting his left ankle in the process. He screamed in pain, but thankfully he had landed on the soft grass, so no other part of his body was injured, but the ankle was damaged and agonising. Nelson quickly followed, and they both tried to run to the nearby road, Darnley being supported by his servant. Behind them they heard shouts as the intruders had burst through the door and seen the chamber empty.

"Get them. They cannot escape, or it be of dire consequence. These traitors must not be at liberty."

"I see them! After them! Afore they reach the road. No-one can look upon them. Run I say. Run!"

Darnley howled in terror as he hobbled across the grass to the sycamore tree that stood between the house and the road. "Help me, for the love of God, help this poor soul!" he shouted, but it was of no avail. The end was quick. They were caught, and in the time that it took the young Darnley to realise that his twenty-two years on this earth was at an end, the rope was around his neck. It took a mere few seconds to choke the life out of him and his only witness, Nelson.

Mary had danced at the marriage of Bastian and Margaret Carwood, as she had promised, but had then retired to her bed early with a tiredness that seemed to drain the very life out of her soul. There was a dullness about the evening, and a sense of doom, but she couldn't understand why it should be more so tonight. She was weary of Darnley, and she didn't know how to deal with him. Keep him close, as she had been advised by all? Divorce him? That would be a difficult task, and surely more ammunition for the firebrand John Knox…and what of Elizabeth? Did she not send Darnley to her as a suitor and did Mary not embrace him and take him for her husband? How could she divorce him so soon afterwards, despite the base and appalling behaviour of the man? It fatigued her deeply, so she closed her eyes trying to get some sleep. As her mind drifted into the moments between waking and sleeping, she saw the vision of Paris, with his face blackened. 'What on earth was he up to?'

At that moment a huge explosion rocked the town. The shock from it lit up the night sky like a firework display, so much so that Mary immediately thought there were festivities in the centre that she hadn't been told about. She rushed to the window and saw in the distance thick black smoke rising high into the sky with red and yellow flames of fire licking at the ground consuming a building. Alarms were set off around her with whistles being blown and soldiers on horses racing to the scene and also surrounding the palace for fear of an attack. Within seconds the people of Edinburgh, also woken up by the enormous blast, were mobilised into action, fearing that their queen had been attacked. Mary watched with astonishment, and then realised, slowly and in total horror, that the explosion had come from Kirk o'Field. To be more exact, it had come from where Darnley was lodged. The building in which she had sat just two hours previously had now been blown sky high, so much so that barely a single stone or rock or wooden beam lay on top of each other. She turned away in distress as her Lady Reres rushed into the room in a state of shock.

"Oh Darnley," was all Mary could utter. "Oh, Henry. What have they done? You did not deserve this," and with that she collapsed to the floor stricken with grief.

Chapter Seven

"Did he do it Mary? Did he say he did it? You have never said." Seton is staring at me and I can see the excitement in her face. She wants to know. She needs to know, but then so do I. Sadly, I don't think I will ever know now. I shake my head slowly.

"I don't know. I really don't. He was accused, and everything pointed to him, but he didn't ever say anything that could bring stains against his character. When I awoke I was told that he had charged down to the scene and taken command. No-one thought the other of him, but it was after when they turned accusers. It was after when we wed that they accused. They painted him the murderer and me the harlot. Such cruel and harsh thoughts, but I swear to you…" I sit up and look at her squarely, "I knew naught of such things. Maybe it was me they wanted dead? I was in the chamber but two hours afore the blast. I was as much in the dark as the grimy face of Paris. I never wished such a horrible death on Henry. I wished him away, of that I will testify, but never the end that befell him. Of that I can swear as the Lord is my judge."

"He was of no noble standing my lady, that is for sure, but a less noble death cannot be imagined. A rope round his neck and his privates showing to all. Why take the time to do him harm if the gunpowder was ready for the same effect? It is of no understanding."

"It is also of no consequence now," I reply sharply. There

is a condescending tone to Seton and I wish it were not so, but then I stop myself and remember that this is the last night I will spend with my oldest friend. "Let us think of Henry in a brighter light." I pull the shawl around my shoulders as the night chill takes hold and look out of the window. In the dark sky I see the twinkling of the stars but the streak of a flash of light. I do not know what it is, but it delights me in its beauty. In a quickening moment, it has gone and the trail of light fades away so that the sky is dark and blemish free again.

"When we first met, Henry was a sweet and young man. He was tender and caring, yet the drink turned him into another. I can forgive his arrogance as he was so young, but his plotting and childish ambition was a knife to my heart. I could not give that part of me to him again. If it were Bothwell who murdered him, there could not have been a more confident man in the kingdom. He strutted around the city and challenged anyone who dare to speak ill of his gains. There is no other man that I could imagine would behave in such a manner. They say I was besotted with him, but they are fools. They say that I followed him and ran to him when he was nearly killed in the borders, but I did what a queen would do. He was my advisor. He was my protector. He was not my assassin."

"Will James know of his father?"

It is a fair question. "It is my wish and my hope that one day James will know the truth of us all. He is a king and he is of my body, so he has the wit and the wisdom to see matters for what they are, and not how they are perceived. I break when I think of my son, yet I hope there is still a light burning somewhere deep inside of him for his mother. I cannot say anymore on the subject. It pains me so…"

"Why did you wed Bothwell?"

The question is as harsh as it is unexpected. For a moment I feel my breath taken away, but I quickly compose myself and think. Why did I? The reason was simple. I had no choice.

"There was little I could do to withstand his advances. His doings were rude, but his words were gentle and kind as well as being strong and protective. He made sure I was protected in my times of need, and he took control so quickly. I needed him. There is no other reason."

"Not love?"

"No, not love. I could not love the man who would abuse me so. I could not fight him, and I could not repeat the doing of it to anyone. Knox would paint me as a whore and Elizabeth would cut me asunder. A queen being forced against her will? How could that be so?"

"He was married! He had mistresses everywhere. What of that woman from Denmark? Anna 'something-or-other.' She had his child! He took the servant girls in the palace whilst he was in your employ. He had pleasures of the flesh aplenty, yet he took you. He took what is precious to us all, and you a queen too. There were too many stories and rumours of him. He had no high morals and he shamed you."

I can do nothing but nod, as I know she is right. Bothwell was an uncouth man, a person whose loyalty was to himself and no other, yet he was also the strongest man I have encountered, and I so desired the strength of such a man in my life. "You are affronted by him and I understand. He was brutish, but he was gentle at times. If it were not for him, I would not have stayed as queen for long, yet because of him I hardly stayed as queen at all. He protected me as he had my dear mother. I cannot reproach him for that."

"He was a rogue my lady. A man of no courtly standing. He disgusted me." Seton slams her fist on the table, making me jump. "I beg your forgiveness Mary, but he angers me so."

"He angered me too my dear Seton, but sometimes…" I allow myself to drift off into a time that is past.

*

Mary and her retinue were riding across the bleak lowlands from Stirling back to Edinburgh. She had been to visit her ten-month-old son James and was now returning with three of her servants and Lord Maitland, plus the usual garrison of soldiers who followed closely behind in protection. The time with her son had disquieted her as she was not allowed to be with him alone. After only an hour in his company, watching him crawl and unsteadily walk in the playroom, he was given back to the care of the Earl of Mar, who was charged with his protection day and night, even against his mother. Mary had inwardly wept that she could not be the person who would watch him grow, watch him learn and see him blossom into a child and then a young man before adulthood. As a queen, these things were not possible. It was her burden, but as a mother, a burden that at times was too much to bear.

The thrill of the ride raised her spirits though. There was no better feeling than to be astride her horse and galloping through the fields, her hair flowing in the wind and her mind cleared of all the stress and worries of the state. Maitland constantly urged her to slow down, but she had the ability of a man in the saddle, and no one would take that from her. She rode through the woods, clearing the overhanging branches with a drop of her head as the others slowed down and fell even further behind. It was exhilarating, and she never felt more alive than in these moments.

"My lady, please stop!" cried Maitland from a distance, his voice betraying both his anxiety and his fatigue in his attempts to keep up. Her guards, seeing that the queen was disappearing into the distance, immediately increased their pace in pursuit, swords and daggers at the ready should any harm befall Mary, but she just continued, completely lost in the moment, and at one stage she let out a scream of pleasure as her horse leapt over a ditch, landing firmly on the opposite bank, keeping his footing without slackening of pace. 'No man can beat me,' she thought. 'I can ride as well as any of them.'

Suddenly she spied a movement in the distance, not more than a couple of hundred yards ahead. It was a group on horseback just at the edge of the path, so that they were half-hidden by the trees. They were standing there with their swords drawn, clearly intent on stopping the queen's progress, maybe five or six men and she couldn't quite make out who was at the head, but as she slowed down to a trot, she saw that it was Bothwell, the Earl. He sat there, lordly and erect with his right arm aloft.

"What is the meaning of this my lord?" demanded Mary, looking behind her and seeing nothing. There was no sign of Maitland or her courtiers and certainly no sign of any of her guards. Suddenly she became afraid, but this was no time to show it. "I am the queen, so pray tell me your business Bothwell."

Bothwell moved forward and put a hand to Mary's horse and calmed it, grabbing the bridle and gently patting its mane. "My lady, I am here to take you away from the danger that awaits you in Edinburgh. I have been told of numerous plots by Moray and his friends against you. They have already gathered an army of over a thousand men and await your return in Edinburgh. You cannot go further as you do not have the protection there that I can afford you here."

Mary looked shocked and confused. "Where are my guards…and Maitland…and my retinue? They were behind me…what have you done?" Her fear was overcoming her.

"Fear not my lady. They are surrounded by my men and they will not be harmed if you agree to follow me. If you do not, then I am sad to say that bloodshed will follow and there will be only one winner." Bothwell stared into her eyes, a glint of fire revealing his ambition and maybe the knowledge that his plan would work quite easily. She sat there, unsure what to do, turning this way and that looking for any of her courtiers, but they were well behind her and presumably being held hostage until a signal from Bothwell. Mary had to weigh up the situation quickly. She could attempt to turn around and bolt, but he was a good rider and would immediately follow. She wouldn't get far. She could call on her guards, but they were too far away, and even if they could hear, they were seemingly in no position to assist, or she could submit and follow him, looking for an opportunity to flee. She needed a clear mind, but her confusion was such that she felt completely lost.

A raindrop fell on her face and looking to the leaden sky,

she saw that the heavy clouds were overhead. "We could stay here all day my lady, but I fear your fair head will soon be drenched and those pretty clothes of yours will soon not be fit to wear." There was no doubt it was said with a leer in his voice, and she noticed him appraising her form.

"Take me to where? On what authority do you have to kidnap the queen?" she demanded, her voice betraying her fear.

"There is no kidnap my lady. This is an errand of mercy. You are in danger and I have always protected you, as I did with your mother. I will lead you to Dunbar and there we will be safe. From then my men will gather and we will retake Edinburgh and place you back on the throne."

"Place me back? Of what do you speak?"

"My lady," Bothwell bowed deferentially, "your brother intends to replace you. He is currently the regent and has already put into place certain plans to ensure you do not return. The uprising is great since the night of your husband. The people blame you, although you do not seem to be aware of such things. There are French placards in the city calling you sundry and foul names and accusing you of murder. Surely you cannot be unaware…?"

"Accusing me!!!" she shouted. "How can that be? I had nothing to do with the foul deed, and may I remind you my lord, that the accusations are heavily weighed against your own person. I have mourned in the correct fashion and I wish that night were not so, but to accuse me of such things is…well it's…treason. That's it, treason!"

"I was acquitted as you know," replied Bothwell, "and I have put up a reward of two thousand pounds for the names of the murderers, but so far there has been nothing…but pray my queen, we tarry too long, for it will rain heavily and we need to depart this place before we are seen by a wondering peasant who would show no loyalty to you or I and would look to the reward of information if he had the chance."

Mary could see no way out of the predicament. Her guards were being detained and if what Bothwell was saying were true, then he was the only man who could protect her. After all, he had never hurt her and had always stood by her side, just as he had with her mother. She nodded in agreement and followed Bothwell and his small group of riders. As they cleared the woods, she looked back and saw that there was an army of a few hundred of his soldiers who were escorting her guards and retinue, Maitland at the head, away from the forest and into the clearing. She shuddered at the thought of what would happen next. Meekly, she turned away and stared at the back of Bothwell, riding purposefully at the head of the group, his stern profile showing that he was totally in command.

Dunbar was a windswept castle on the east coast of the country, unchanged for over a hundred years since the last attempted French invasion. It was a place she had visited many times, delighting in the stories of 'Black Agnes', the Countess of Dunbar, who two centuries earlier had stood firm against the English invaders and even swept the battlements at night with her handkerchief in preparation for the next day's skirmishes. It was a wonderful story that she liked to read and reread every time she came to the castle, and she often wondered if there was a memory of her life that would be retold in the years to come. 'Perchance not' she thought. 'I will be forgotten the moment I depart this world. There will be few who will keep my memory alive.' It saddened her. As did the castle she was approaching.

Now Dunbar looked foreboding and gloomy and as she rode into the wide courtyard, she looked around her and saw little to cheer. Bothwell's guards stood at the entrance and the large brazier in the centre flickered and danced as the eastern winds gusted around. As she got down from her steed, she had to keep her hair from becoming unruly and her skirts from riding up her legs as the heavy breeze caught her. No soldier should be allowed to see a queen in disarray.

She was shown to her apartment. It was small, on the second floor reached by a small staircase, and had none of the trappings of royalty. The bed was bare of any adornments, but there were two feather pillows and a thick set of blankets, plus the fire was burning brightly in the hearth, giving a warm glow and some needed heat to the room. Bothwell followed after. He seemed amused to be there.

"I trust this will be sufficient my lady, although I fear it is of nought when compared to your bed chambers, which I am assured are of a luxury that few can match." He smirked. Mary looked at him in surprise and a degree of shock.

"Whatever you have heard of my private chambers, you can definitely be assured that these are of far inferior quality. How long do you intend to keep me here?"

"I do not keep you ma'am. You are free to leave as and when you wish, but there is a danger that you must not take lightly. We will abode here for a few days until the time my army is great enough to return to the task at hand."

Mary sat down on the small stool by the fire, welcoming the heat that warmed her chilled body. "I am here under protest, and be assured my Earl, that should there be any deception in your doings, then the punishment will be great. I am rather hungry and thirsty after my ride. Please bring me a meal and drink."

Bothwell bowed and then pulled out a document from the pouch that was attached to his waist. "I will order my servant to bring you food and ale. There is no wine here I'm afraid…and I would like you to peruse this my lady."

She took the parchment and unrolled it. "What is it?"

"Please read it. It is the proof of my innocence, something you have questioned already this day."

She waited for him to leave the room, noticing that he locked it from the outside and then opened the parchment and read.

'James, Earl of Bothwell, being calumniated by malicious reports and divers placards as art and part in the heinous murder of the king, has submitted to an assize, and been found innocent of the same by certain noblemen his peers and other barons of good reputation. We, the undersigned…'

She looked to the foot of the document and saw the signatures of twenty-eight nobles and lords who were of sympathy to the Earl, including that of Maitland, her so-called trusted advisor. 'How did he get all of these people to sign this?' she wondered. 'What kind of trickery is this?' She moved closer to the flames so as to give light to the paper and read on…

'oblige ourselves upon our faith and honour and truth of our bodies, will answer to God, that in case hereafter any

manner of persons shall happen to insist further on the slander of the said heinous murder we and our kin, friends and assisters, shall take true and plain part with him to the defence and maintenance of his quarrel with our bodies, heritage and goods...'

It was a declaration of innocence that *he* had written and somehow had forced everyone to sign. This was no proof of acquittal but a document of subterfuge. He had been found not guilty of Darnley's murder in a trial that belonged more to the mummeries and festivities of the court than to any real justice, and now this! Then she read the most disturbing part....

'and as Her Majesty is now destitute of husband, in which solitary state the Commonwealth cannot permit Her Highness to continue, if it should please her so far to humble herself by taking one of her own born subjects and marry the said Earl, we will maintain and fortify him against all who would hinder and disturb the said marriage. Under our hands and seals at Edinburgh this day of April the 19th in the year 1567'

"Oh, my dear God," cried Mary as she let the parchment fall from her trembling hands to the floor. "Oh God, what have I done? I know why I am here. This is not for my safety. I have been kidnapped. The door is locked, I cannot leave. I am a prisoner. Oh, my dear God save me. What is to become of me now?" and she put her head in her hands and wept. She had been tricked.

*

"My darling Mary..." Seton says, looking at me with tears in her eyes. "I wish I had been there to help you."

"There was nothing you could do, or indeed anyone. He

was too strong and determined. It was his ambition. I had no hope of being able to stop him. He had planned it all along."

Seton seems to struggle to find the words. "He took you…he took you…by force?"

I nod. There is a silence. I don't want to relive that evening, but it had happened. After a while I look back at her and explain. "I remember the look in his eyes when he walked into the room. He'd been drinking, but he was clear-eyed and steady on his feet. I don't recall what I said, but I know I tried to hide behind the bed and then made for the door, but he was too strong. I shouted and screamed, but no-one would come to my aid, there were none of my guards or servants, none of my friends…" I catch Seton looking at me and regretted what I'd just said.

"None of my friends who had ridden with me that day" I reassure her. "I was helpless. Helpless like a rabbit caught in the snare, except the rabbit's end must surely have been preferable than to my next few moments."

"You don't have to carry on…"

Oh, my dear Seton, still caring for me after all these years, and now on my final night. Has there ever been a more loyal and trusted friend. What will you do once I have gone? What will you do tomorrow?

"Do not worry. It is in the past, but I still recall it as if it was the yesterday." I sit up and look in her eyes. Now you deserve the truth. The truth that I have hidden all these years.

"Once the deed was done, he got up and straightened his clothes and looked down at me as if I was a servant girl. He was smiling, but it was a cruel smile. I was dishevelled, and

I wanted to be sick, but the bile wouldn't come. My head was hurting as if it had been banged against the wall and there was a pain..." I swallow, take a breath, and continue, "and all he said was that now I had to marry him as I was his. He'd ravished me, and no queen could stand the despair or the shame and so it had to be so. He would be my king. I couldn't say against his wishes. He was right. How could I continue? If I didn't agree then the rumours would be everywhere. He would spread them. He would tell the lords of my base behaviour, how I begged him. He would tell Knox of how I was a harlot and Elizabeth would learn of it...I couldn't argue against him. Do you see now why I couldn't tell a soul? Do you see now why I had but of no choice but to marry? The shame was too great...too great"

I refuse to cry. On my last night, I will not cry again. This is my life. There will be no more tears.

Chapter Eight

On the night of her third marriage, Mary did cry. She cried with a sadness that she hadn't felt since the loss of Francois, except this time she cried privately. There was no-one, except her Maries, who would be allowed to see the despair that she was in.

The wedding had been a quick and understated affair. Holyrood was hardly adorned for the ceremony, and as it was conducted in Protestant fashion, it barely registered with Mary. She walked through it in a daze, but she had at least taken Mass in the morning. She stood there as the pronouncements were made and hardly listened to a word. All she could think about was how she had come to be in this place, wedding the man who was accused of murdering her second husband. At one stage she'd turned her head to look at Bothwell as they listened to the marriage vows, and a small shudder went through her body. The memory of the night, and the many nights since, when he had forced himself upon her, was too visible. The shudder was for another reason though. Was it possible that his roughness and crudeness had awakened something in her? She didn't want to be married to this man, but she knew that if she wanted to keep the crown, then such a man would be there to protect her and fight for her. In an odd way, it made him slightly less undesirable…

Later that evening, sat alone in her private chamber whilst her new husband was celebrating with his lords, she wrote a letter. She had to somehow convey her unhappiness to someone, even if it were to stand witness in years to come, that this was not a marriage she'd entered willingly. There was only one person she could trust to read it and keep for future posterity, the Bishop of Dunblane.

'As envy follows virtues, and this country is of itself somewhat subject to factions, others begin to mislike his proceeding, and so far by reports and misconstructing his doings, went about to put him out of our good grace. He obtained a writing subscribed with all their hands, wherein they not only granted their consent to our marriage with him, but also obliged them to set him forward with their lives and goods. This realm being divided in factions as it is, cannot be contained in order, unless our authority be assisted and forthset by the fortification of a man who must take upon his person in the execution of justice. The travail thereof we may no longer sustain in our own person, being already wearied, and almost broken with the frequent uproars and rebellions raised against us since we came to Scotland.'

She wanted to write more, oh such more, but the words failed her. She wanted to cry out in anger and tell the bishop of how she was kidnapped and held captive, ravished and forced into this unholy union, but as a queen, she knew she could not. She knew anything written regarding her husband would be used against him, either now or in some day future, and she would be useless without him at her side. The dilemma was great, but deep down she also trusted the bishop to be a pious and intelligent man, and hopefully he would have the ability to read what had not been written, as well as the words that were drying on the parchment. With a heavy sigh, she rolled up the letter, sealed it with wax, stamped her royal insignia and called for her servant to deliver with haste. All she could do then would be to wait. Wait for Bothwell to join her in the matrimonial bed and wait for the winds to change in her favour.

The next day she was informed that Maitland had chosen to leave her court, without even a farewell to the woman he had served for so long. His dislike of Bothwell, and his anger over the kidnapping of the queen, had not subsided and he felt there was no choice but to depart. It put Mary into even more of a distressed state.

"There is but no-one left for me now," she wailed to Jane. "This man has taken everything from me, even though he professes to love and honour me."

"My lady, the Earl has always made his intentions clear in that regard. Why just today the news of his divorce from Jean has been ratified by the court. He wants you and you alone, but for what reasons, we cannot tell at this time. You must stay strong Mary. It is our only hope."

"Divorce! I never asked him to divorce. I never asked him to marry me. I never asked for any of this. I suppose my name will be mentioned in the papers for the annulment too."

"It is not my queen, and we can be thankful for that. It is the young lass Bessie who is cited. It seems she was one of his many…mistresses."

Mary looked at her with horror. "I should be thankful that my husband is carrying on with a scullery maid? Oh, the shame of all of this. Will this never end?"

"He will honour and protect you and the realm within.

There cannot be a better match at this time."

"Have you too been bewitched by this man? How can you say there is no better match? I do not love him, and I do not desire him. If only my dear Francois was still alive…"

Sadly, he was no longer. Neither was Riccio or Darnley or King Henry of France or her dear mother Mary of Guise, or indeed were there any signs of life from the many people who had professed to serve her as queen yet had now all but disappeared. Maitland was the latest.

The one man who had promised to serve her as queen, was the one man who now abused her position for his own gains. Bothwell never loved Mary, of that there was no doubt. He loved his wife Jean, who he'd had to divorce, but more than any woman, he loved his ambition. To be married to the Queen of Scotland, to take the regency, the Crown Matrimonial, to confer on himself the titles and the estates without challenge, was his dream realised. He would always take care of Mary, his natural demeanour meant that no man would challenge him, and he would not harm her in any way, despite his actions in Dunbar, but she was made aware that this was a marriage of convenience. She was his now. No court decision or proclamation was made without his authority, no manifesto was delivered without his stamp or seal, and no uprising or insurrection was dealt with without his ruthlessness. Mary was now effectively a redundant queen. She was not consulted or approached. She was not listened to or welcomed in the area of government and her seal of office was replaced by the seal of Bothwell, so that she now couldn't even sign an official document. As each day passed, she felt she was fading away, unnoticed by all around her. The once glorious queen, with her legendary beauty, was now a shuffling figure who appeared at mealtimes in the dining-hall and then returned to whence she came.

Despite all of this, she still felt a sense of bond growing with Bothwell. She wasn't falling in love as she felt it would be impossible to fall for such a brute, but the responsibility of state was being removed from her shoulders, and the weight was no longer a burden. She no longer had to concern herself with her realm, and with each day free from decision-making a sense of attachment grew with her husband. His nightly demands became less of a chore, and she even found herself idly concerning over his numerous mistresses. It wasn't jealousy, she was sure, but a need to know that he was always going to be her king, and not abandon her like all of the rest. With so many of her loved ones dying, Bothwell was the one, strong person who surely would never die? She would always be safe, and in turn Scotland would always be safe. The contract or convenience or arrangement of the marriage was beginning to work, and she no longer felt it untoward.

As for Bothwell? He continued to see Jean, and he continued to see Bess. He also continued to see any lass that he fancied, but he too was becoming aware of a longing for Mary, far beyond the initial reason. She was weak and vulnerable. She was powerless as a queen now, and she was prone to many emotional moments, but he was a man and he would take care of his wife. With this understanding, the two began to imagine the life that would follow.

*

"I have never had the time to look back on my life," I say to Seton. "I've never learned the art of contemplation as everything passed by so quickly. I was playing a part in a play, but now the final act is here, and I don't seem to have the time anymore."

Seton looks at me with that same image of concern that she has had for so long. I wonder how she will cope once I am gone? It is dark now and the shadows are flickering across her face. The candle is strong and bright, but it gives out no heat and I feel my fingertips throb with the pain of the cold. Seton obviously sees this and immediately gets up from her stool and crosses to the door.

"Where are you going?"

"I am asking the lord if he will allow a fire to be lit on this final evening. He cannot deny this wish. It is too cold here and you do not deserve to have this hardship inflicted upon you at this late hour."

I am inclined to protest but think better of it. She is right. I do not deserve to spend my last evening in the chill of a winter's night, but my hopes are not high for her success. I also think of her words – *this late hour* – a metaphor perhaps? Whatever she meant, it was true, this was this late hour, and for me the lateness is increasing. I sit there, wishing away the cold, but also knowing that I will not do such a thing again, and think of the warmth and the heat and the sunshine of my time in France. I miss France so. What I would give to be back in its embrace, to feel the loving arms of the royal court, the sensuous feel of the scandal that engulfed it every day, the freedom of the chase on horseback, the gaiety of the summer fetes and the warm caress of my dear Francois. The dauphin, a child but my dearest and most loving companion. Where did those days go? Does Francois look down on me with tears in his eyes as he sees his Marie living in this prison fortress, ready to be executed? Does he not cry out in anger and despair at my incarceration? Is he disappointed in me like so many others? Is he ashamed at my actions? Is he there? Does he wait for my arrival? I was told by Paulet that I will go to hell, but I am convinced there is a place reserved for me in heaven, albeit one that has not always been available. If it is hell though, I will reserve a special type of misery for my detractors and traitors, but if it is heaven, then I would gladly spend all of my time there with dear Francois.

The door opens, and Seton enters with a special guard of the palace. He bows deferentially to me, and I return the gesture. It is fine of him and I appreciate it.

"Your fire will be lit this final evening," says Seton gaily. She is smiling, and I wonder inwardly what she has had to do to persuade him to act. There was not enough time for the lords to receive my request and consider it, so she must have spoken to the first guard she saw. It worked, and I suddenly feel happier as the guard puts to work the kindling and the heavy logs and lighting them with the touch paper. In seconds the flames begin to rise from the grate and immediately there is a warmth to the air.

"My lord I thank-you. You have done me a kindness and I will remember this to the end. Pray tell me, what is your name guard?"

He stands erect and looks me in the eye. "I am James Farfield my lady. By Order of the Queen's Guards my job is to protect you whilst you reside here at Fotheringhay. I hope and pray that I have been assistance to you." Again, he bows deeply, and I am touched. I reach and place my hand on his shoulder.

"You say you pray. Who do you pray to my guard and by what faith?"

"I pray to the one God who bestows his blessings on our life. I pray by the faith of the Roman church, if you may…"

I let him stand and I mark the cross on his forehead. He is a fine figure of a man, a gentle but strong face with a full beard and deep, dark brown eyes. In a way, standing in his full armoury with his dagger in its sheath and his breastplate shining in the flicker of the flames, he reminds me briefly of Bothwell. The same sensuous mouth, the same pronounced nose and the same tuft of thick hair protruding from his steel cap. I am for a moment quite taken-aback, and allow myself to believe that it is him, but of course that would be foolish. This is no time for such fantasies.

"My dear soldier. Go in peace and I will pray for your safety as I bid you all farewell. God be with you." He nods at me slowly and then smiles before turning and leaving. It was only a momentary encounter, but it makes me realise that all is not hurt and pain in this world, but that there are those who do good and think good. If only I'd been fortunate enough to have met more in my life!

I return to the stool opposite Seton and we sit silently in the warmth of the fire. It's quite an oddity that despite my only having a few hours to live, the sight and the feel of a burning hearth can lift the spirits. Suddenly the shawl no longer feels necessary and I can feel my cheeks burning with the heat coming from the logs. Seton is the first to speak.

"He reminded you of him, didn't he Mary?"

"He did…yes he did," I answer almost in a whisper. "I never thought I would think of Bothwell as much as I have this evening, but he seems to be all around me. You knew who to ask didn't you?" My tone is grave but teasing and Seton immediately replies in a mockingly defensive way.

"Oh but of course not. It never occurred to me…"

We laugh together, and I know how much I love this friend sat with me in my final hours. Of all the companions I have had, she is the one who has always been there. My dear Seton…

"He should have stayed by your side. He should never have left. I cannot forgive him for leaving you.", she suddenly exclaims, surprising me with her force. "It wasn't enough that he fled at Borthwick, but then to do the same at Carberry Hill, is unforgiveable. I know I could never forgive him, and even if he has survived his prison cell in Denmark, I will still hope for his death."

"I understand. In my heart of hearts, I want to believe that he had found a way to love me, as I tried to love him, but it was to no avail." I try to be soothing with my words and tone, but there is still an anger deep inside me that refuses to go. "He had one ambition and he would do what he needed to achieve it, yet sometimes I saw in him a bravery, a courage that was not just on the battlefield, but between us. There was a glimpse that he was willing to forgo his mistresses and his greed and his avarice for my love, but I could never give him that love…eventually he abandoned me."

"You must not think that way my lady!" exclaims Seton angrily. "Whatever the tides of history wash up in the future, you and I must always remember that this man forced you into marriage when you were at your most vulnerable. He took away your crown. He took away your freedom and he took away your own son. He abandoned you because he was Bothwell, not because of your perceived lack of love for him. He was a rogue, a brute and a coward. He left you in the hands of the lords and he never returned. Never. Do you hear me my lady? He never returned!"

*

"We have an army. We can fight them. I know what I am doing in the battlefield so help me God. This is the right place and the right time." Bothwell sat astride his horse at the foot of Carberry Hill, his army stretched behind him all the way to the peak. He had two hundred harquebusiers, six hundred horsemen, a thousand savage borderers ready to attack at a moment's notice and a further two thousand unarmed villagers scattered amongst the fighting men. There were brass field guns positioned at strategic places on the hillside, and to all its purposes, the army looked strong and resistant. As did Bothwell. He sat there, ever in command and a man as comfortable in this position as an eagle is on a branch ready to swoop at its prey. Next to him stood the flapping red and yellow lion royal standard flag, with another, the cross of St Andrew, behind him. Bothwell looked resplendent in his armour, a complete contrast to poor Mary. She sat alongside him in her men's clothes and the too small red petticoat, that she'd had to take as part of her disguise when she had set to flee Borthwick. With her hair shaved short, her legendary beauty was hidden, yet still every man in the army looked upon her with desire and lust, knowing that such treasonous thoughts could get them killed in an instant. The unswerving loyalty was something she had always been able to rely on.

"Our armies are evenly matched though?" she asked in concern as she surveyed the scene not more than half a mile in front of her. "We must stand a chance with all of these men behind us. I can see the Earl of Morton and the Earl of Home. They have huge numbers my love. Huge numbers…"

"Fear not Mary. Our numbers are evenly matched as you say, and yes they do have better weapons and a cavalry to call on, but they don't have *me!*"

Mary carried on staring at the army facing her and to her horror she saw that the Highlanders had arrived, boosting their numbers. They were trained in battle and the unarmed and scared villagers who made up her numbers could hardly be expected to fight them.

"Do you know where we are…?" asked Bothwell almost casually. He'd also seen the Highlanders arrive but had decided to pay no heed. Mary looked around and shook her head. "We are near Pinkie Clough, the scene of the battle that sent you to France when you were a child. I was there, but I did no fighting as I was but a young boy of twelve. I watched from afar, but I swore that one day you would be avenged. Now is that day…"

It didn't make Mary feel any better. She knew how loyal Bothwell had been to her mother's cause and she knew on the battlefield she could rely on him, but there was a gloomy feeling in her stomach. It was tied in knots and she couldn't help herself in believing that this confrontation would not end well. The day was already long, and the sun was rising. The men hadn't brought provisions as they were told there would be a brief skirmish and it would be at an end. In fact, they had been told they would march triumphantly into Edinburgh and place Mary back on the throne. There was no suggestion that they would face an army this size, or indeed an army of any size.

She looked amongst the faces opposite her on the hill facing Carberry, and tried to find her half-brother James, the new regent. As if Bothwell could read her mind, he said forcefully. "You won't find Moray. He is never around when there is trouble. I have it on good authority that he is in northern France eating for all his worth, awaiting the signal for his return. I intend that signal never to be given."

"I see the murderers of Riccio are back. There is Lord Ruthven..." she said pointing in the distance "and Lord Lindsay...and oh, Erskine. Oh, not Erskine. He is my son's keeper. How could he have turned so?" The tinge of betrayal stung her.

"Aye lass. They have all turned. We'll have their heads!" It was Bothwell at his most bullish. He was made for moments like this. "Look Mary, there at the head of the group of the front horsemen. Do you see the banner?"

Mary looked and yes, she saw in her horror and despair the banner that was held aloft for all to see. It was of white satin and had the drawn figures of Darnley and the baby boy James with the words 'judge and avenge my cause, O Lord' underneath. Almost as if the soldier who was holding it could see her eyes, he held it higher and the horsemen behind gave a cry that sounded like 'burn the whore!', but the wind swept away the clarity, so that Mary was left distressed and confused.

"They will all die for this treason," shouted Bothwell, as much to his men as to Mary who was close by. "We have the advantage. They will not attack up the hill. We have too many defensive strongholds for them. They would be foolish. As soon as Huntly and Hamilton arrive, we will force upon them and they will scurry like mice…"

Unfortunately for Bothwell and Mary, neither Huntly nor Hamilton and their men appeared. Whatever promises had been given, were broken at the time of importance. As they and the men waited, the sun became hotter and the army behind them became restless. The soldiers were itching for battle, as after all that is what they are trained for. To stand still and wait is torture to a battled horseman. The others, especially the villagers, began to get concerned. They were thirsty and hungry, and the heat was sapping their strength as well as their commitment. One by one they deserted, running into the woods behind so as not to be seen. It was Mary who firstly saw the foolhardiness of their situation.

"We cannot win. Our men are bored and listless. They cannot stand much longer."

Bothwell nodded. "I could march some of them southward and try and get more ground advantage, but we are now outnumbered. It would be of no assistance." He looked around and saw that his army was dwindling fast. In the distance he watched as around a dozen villagers threw down their pitchforks and other 'weapons' they had brought with them and scampered into the woods. 'They were of little use anyhow,' he thought. The situation was now dire. He knew, as a military strategist, that this battle could not be won today, but he had an idea. There was one way it *could* be won. If he challenged any man to hand-to-hand combat, then there would be no bloodshed on Carberry Hill today and he was convinced that there was no-one that was of a skill like his.

"I challenge any man to meet me in a neutral place and take me on single-handedly. That way we can avoid the battle!" he shouted across the field. His words were heard, but no-one heeded them. Every soldier in the lord's encampment knew of the skill that the Earl had in hand-to-hand combat, and there was not a one of them who relished taking up the challenge…

Instead the day grew long, and the sun rose higher in the sky. Mary felt weary and not a little faint from the hours of inactivity sat in the saddle. Her horse was restless and scraped its hooves on the grass in frustration. Everyone sat and waited, except those who turned to leave. Bothwell espied two old farmers who had decided they wanted no more of the endeavour and had turned back into the woods.

"Blaggards both of you! Cursed is every man who betrays the queen. I will have your heads…," but he did not move. He too seemed to be weighed down by the stand-off. The air was heavy with despondency and soon it was becoming clear to both Mary and Bothwell that there was no way forward to victory. Behind them, their army had reduced itself to a mere few hundred, whilst opposite them sat the massed forces of the lords. Any battle now would inevitably be lost. A cooling breeze appeared which fluttered the flags and gave a small comfort to the men who were hot, hungry and thirsty, but it also signalled the end of the day, when soon it would be nightfall.

"How long have we waited?" asked Mary.

"Surely nine, maybe ten hours. Soon it will be dark, and we can surprise them," replied Bothwell, but his tone was that of hope as opposed to commitment.

"Look…" Mary pointed at two riders approaching in the

gathering gloom. "Is that not du Croc, the French ambassador and Kirkcaldy? What are they about?"

"If it is a trick, it is a poor one. Be aware everyone!" he shouted as much to himself as the men behind him. He pulled his dagger free from its sheath and sat ready to receive them both.

It was du Croc who arrived first and spoke.

"Madam, Sir…" he bowed elegantly whilst still sat astride his horse. "I have agreed to mediate in this dispute, so I arrive with no allegiance and I take no side. The Lord Kirkcaldy is here to ensure that all words between us are reported back fairly. He is fluent in French as you know."

"What of it?" demanded Bothwell, his hand still on his dagger.

"I would prefer there not to be bloodshed on this day, and it would be a shame if it were so after such a long stand-off. I am here purely as a mediator." Bothwell nodded in agreement and returned the dagger back to its sheath at his belt. The ambassador continued.

"I am instructed to tell you that the lords will look favourably on you my lady, if you were to abandon your husband and let him depart from this place. I am told also, that they would be willing to act on your behalf to eventually return you to the throne should you turn your back on this marriage. They are willing servants of the queen and have only one wish, that is to have the rightful heir wearing her crown."

Mary sat shocked, but surprised. She said nothing, but Bothwell immediately reacted in anger. "Are they not the same lords who signed the bond to confirm my marriage to the queen? Did they not agree to defend our cause with their lives?"

"That may be so," responded Kirkcaldy with a strong tone of voice, "but that bond was signed under duress and with the help of large quantities of ale and wine, as you know."

Mary looked at Bothwell. This was the first she'd known of such a thing. He continued to stare at the two men. "No man will tell the Earl of Bothwell what his mind is. I will not be run through from the battlefield."

"Unless you leave immediately, we cannot ensure your safety, or our lady or any of your men," said du Croc in a gentle manner. "Your grace must see that this battle would be lost this day for you all. Your men are leaving, and your army is demoralised and outnumbered. We have been watching for most of the day. It was a surprise to the lords that you did not make your move at the noon-time when there was still an advantage."

Again, Mary turned to look at Bothwell. His face was stern and betrayed no fear. He looked like he was ready to pounce at a moment's notice, yet had he not warned that his army was not ready until reinforcements arrived? Those same reinforcements that are still absent?

"Can you guarantee safe passage for my lord?" she demanded, much to the surprise of them all. She felt a waft of breeze play on her cheek and looking to the sky saw a black cloud gradually move over the spot where they were all standing. Soon it would rain, and her army would almost certainly desert her then.

"I cannot," replied du Croc, "but I will say that he will not be attacked whilst he is in view on the battlefield. Only once the earl has left, will he be pursued. There is nothing I can offer that is fairer than that."

"And what of my demands? Will you take me to Edinburgh and allow me to sit on the throne that is rightfully mine and was taken from me in such a cruel and heartless fashion?"

Du Croc bowed again deferentially. "I have been given their assurance that you will be taken from this spot madam, but only once the earl has departed."

Mary sat and thought. What to do? The day was lost, even she knew that. How could she let Bothwell go? He has been by her side and is her only protector. She stared at his features. He had said nothing for a few minutes and sat there, his right hand holding the reins of his horse and the other hovering near the dagger, as if he was ready to take on both of them and rip their stomachs open. There was a sense of anger in his demeanour, but she also saw something else. Was he thinking of the offer? He looked deep in thought, and she wondered. Would he be prepared to leave her?

"You must go my husband. It is the only way. There is nothing to be gained from this anymore. We can regroup and fight another day, especially once I am back as the rightful queen."

Bothwell hesitated and then turned to look at her. "I won't be forced away like a sheep runs from the shepherd. I came for battle." The words were strong, but they were delivered in a monotone voice.

"You see this is hopeless? I am giving you leave to depart my lord. There will be no bloodshed this day and I hope to avoid seeing yours. Do you understand?" She was testing him. Testing his resolve. Was it as strong?

"I will return with an army twice this size and I will sit at your right hand as king." The words were said without emotion.

So, there it was. Her Bothwell, the fine, brave and fearless warrior, who had slain men for insults, commanded armies and faced his accusers in Edinburgh face-to-face after Darnley's murder with barely a hint of fear, was now itching to flee the battlefield and leave her alone at the mercy of the lords. Suddenly it was clear to her. He had never loved her. He wouldn't protect her. He only wanted her for the regency.

"Farewell my lord," and she leaned over to kiss him on the cheek. He reached into his breast pocket and pulled out a piece of paper. "Read this when you're alone. It explains everything…" and with that he patted her cheek with his hand, turned and rode off towards the woods. Mary watched and wondered if she would ever see him again.

It was only a few days later when she read the note that she realised that he'd had no intention of fighting the battle, that in fact he'd planned to escape, albeit by different means to the one that took place.

'Do not fear. Stay strong and I will return on the morrow with a thousand fighting soldiers to your cause. My loving Mary. your loving James'

She had been betrayed again.

She also realised very quickly that she had been betrayed by both du Croc and Kirkcaldy. There was no safe passage for her. The moment Bothwell had disappeared, their army dispersed and retreated back into the woods, and she was led by her horse down Carberry Hill and to the head of the lords' army. There she was greeted by Morton, Ruthven and Atholl. All looked at her with contempt. As she was led slowly through the lines of soldiers, she heard murmurs as they parted to let her through. Her blood ran cold. Whispers at first, said by a few, and then like a crescendo the whole garrison started screaming 'Burn her! Burn the whore! Burn the murderess!!'

Mary was terrified and called out to Kirkcaldy. "I am the queen and you gave me your promise."

"I gave no promise madam. You will be safe though. The men will not harm you whilst I am here, but you are being led to your rightful place indeed. You will be imprisoned and tried for the murder of your second husband, our king, Darnley."

Mary was rigid with fear. The banner that she'd seen earlier was now held before her as she was escorted off the hill and onto the road towards the city. The men near her made ribald comments about her dress, noticing how her ankles showed below the filthy red petticoat she had been forced to wear for two days. They made lude and aggressive suggestions to her, as if she was a lady walking the streets of the old town. One reached out to try to touch her breasts, but Morton quickly intervened and demanded that no man should lay a finger on her on pain of death. Still the shouts and insults continued.

"I am the queen! You must respect me!!" but that was met with even more ridicule and whoops of laughter followed by disgusting remarks. It was the longest journey in her life.

As they entered the city by way of the tolbooth, she was firstly lifted by the sight of people crowding the streets, presumably to welcome back their sovereign, but whatever hope she had was dashed immediately. Her heart sunk once again when she heard the cries of 'Murderess!' and 'Witch' aimed at her. These same people who had welcomed her as queen but only six years ago, and who had been devoted to her, now threw insults and profanities as she passed by. Some even threw objects, and she had to duck as a tomato hit her on the arm, splashing its red liquid over her bodice. Morton and Kirkcaldy looked concerned, and it was to their credit that they managed to protect Mary from the wrath of the crowd, before scurrying her into the inn, where a room had been made ready for her arrival.

"We are not to go to the castle?" she asked weakly, after sitting down on the edge of the bare bed exhausted.

"No. As you can see, it is too dangerous. We will move you elsewhere tomorrow," replied Morton.

"Why did you lie to me?"

"My lady, why did you lie to us?"

Chapter Nine

I open my eyes suddenly. I can't bear the memories. I shake my head violently as if that very act will banish the images that are there. I don't want to remember. I don't want to think about the agony of that evening and the despair I felt. I can't bring myself to think of the anger on the faces of the people below, or the betrayal as the ones I trusted walked by and pretended not hear my cries. I was told that I tore my dress open, bared myself and screamed from the window, yet those memories are not mine.

I have no recollection of the journey to Edinburgh Castle and my brief stay there, yet I was told that we stayed but for one evening. All I recall was the boat and the long and silent journey across the cold lake and to my first prison, Lochleven. It was twenty-years ago now, yet I remember the chill I felt as if it were yesterday as I was led up the tiny grass hill and into the castle, a place I knew so well. I'd entertained princes and courtiers there, and even had heated arguments with that firebrand Knox there, and yes, I'd spent long blissful hours with Henry there. My senses were alive to the sounds and sights of life when I was with him at that time. The sky was clearer, the grass was greener, the larks sang more beautifully, and the lavender's aroma was stronger, yet on that day the castle towered above me in grey and gloom. Those moments….

Seton is sitting in the corner of the room. She is quiet and I at this moment prefer it that way. She is distracting herself with needlework, and I wish I had the desire to join her. The nights we two would sit and darn and talk and gossip. That is for no more now, and with the hour getting late, I decided I have to start my correspondence. There are many who I need to write to, and whilst I still have my wits, I should make a beginning. I unroll the scroll, pick up the quill and begin. It is to my beloved brother-in-law in France, King Henry;

'Today, after dinner, I was advised of my sentence. I am to be executed like a criminal at eight o' clock in the morning. I haven't had enough time to give you a full account of all that has happened, but if you will listen to my physician and my other sorrowful servants, you will know the truth, and how, thanks be to God, I scorn death and faithfully protest that I face it innocent of any crime...'

Innocent of any crime. Will they believe me? I did nothing wrong. I made mistakes, I was hasty, and I was rash, but who hasn't regretted a moment that was borne out of passion? I did not participate in the murder of Darnley, and I did not take Riccio as my lover as has been said. I did neither of those things...yet I am accused. I am accused of plotting to kill Elizabeth, but I did not willingly entertain any such thoughts...yet I am accused. I continue...

'the Catholic faith and the defence of my God-given right to the English throne are the two reasons for which I am condemned, and yet they will not allow me to say that it is for the Catholic faith that I die. I beg you as Most Christian Majesty, my brother-in-law and old friend, who have always protested your love for me, to give proof now of your kindness on all these points, both by paying charitably my unfortunate servants their arrears of wages, and also by

having prayers offered to God for a Queen who has herself been called Most Christian, and who dies a Catholic, stripped of all her possessions. Concerning my son, I commend him to you inasmuch as he deserves it, as I cannot answer for him. I venture to send you two precious stones, amulets against illness, trusting that you will enjoy good health and a long and happy life. Your loving Marie'

The writing has exhausted me, yet there are so many more letters I need to compose. For some reason I suddenly remember the moment the steel blade touched my bare neck as Moray threatened me unless I signed the abdication papers. Why was I cursed with such an unloving brother? Was his ambition of such that he would gladly slay his sister for the clothing of kingdom? Even now, so many years later, I can feel the point pierce my skin slightly as he stood over me. Then I move forward and the see the sneers of the guards as I watch the fireworks explode from the courtyard of Lochleven. They are celebrating a new King. My son, James, barely old enough to walk, and now the ruler of Scotland, yet not the ruler at all. No, that was Moray, the bastard son who with his scheming, took my crown. I am Queen though. I am the Queen of Scotland and her Isles. Even now, on my last evening, I can say that I am the Queen.

There is a knock on the door.

"My lady. It is I Willie. May I enter?"

Willie Douglas. Willie who has stayed with me all these years since he helped me escape at Lochleven. Of all my retinue, no matter how small it is now, he is the one who will take this the hardest and with despair. I steel myself.

"Enter my dear friend," and the door opens and there is

Willie. He looks quite ill. His face is red and puffy, and his demeanour suggests he has been crying. "Willie, come to me."

He walks to me unsteadily and I wonder if he has been drinking? It would not be like him, but then these are times when we can behave in unusual ways. I stay seated, mainly because it pains me to stand too quickly, and for that reason he towers above me. I notice his shirt is rumpled and has come loose from his breeches and the scarf he always wears around his neck is hanging loose. I hold out my hands and he takes them gently. "Crouch down so that I don't strain my neck looking up at this fine manly specimen."

I know he loves these compliments and I would be blind not to see that he has been in love with me ever since we fled Lochleven all those years ago. For twenty years this man has been at my side, never wavering in his devotion to me, sharing the same prisons and captivity as me, and all for a love that could never be reciprocated. I always hoped he understood that.

"Willie..." I talk softly to him as I can see just the hint of a tear in his eye, "it is time to say goodbye. Please don't cry for me my dear, dear Willie. You have been my trusted friend for all of these years and I have always kept you in my heart." I see him smile, and as yet he hasn't spoken. "I know what your feelings have been, and trust me, if it were not for the misfortune of our births, I too would have shown you the same love as you have shown me. I want you to know that," and I allow him to kiss my hand. I stroke his neck and see his eyes close before I feel the shaking of his shoulders as the tears fall. At that moment I hold him to my bosom for the first and last time in my life and I allow him to sob into my dress. No one is here to see except Seton and she keeps her eyes deliberately lowered. This is the one act of kindness I can do for the man who has stood by me and will continue to stand by me.

"You must promise me something." I take his hands and look at him. He nods, his tears still falling. "When I am gone, you must travel to France and see the king. There you will deliver my letter to him. Ask him to do all that is requested and to ensure that all of my possessions, meagre that they are, be divided fairly between my courtiers. I also ask that you make arrangements for my coach and horses to be sold and the proceeds to be given to Seton, Jane and my ladies, so that they have passage to wherever they may desire to go."

Willie nods again. It is a lot to ask, but I know he won't fail me. "Anything you desire my lady."

"There is one more thing I may ask of you…" I look at him and then to Seton, "of both of you."

"Anything," replies Willie and Seton stops her needlework and pays attention.

"I have not been given the courtesy of having my chaplain in my last hours, and I will not die proclaiming the Protestant faith, so I need to give my confession before the face of God. I'd like you both to be my witnesses."

Willie lowers his head, his hands still in mine, and Seton comes to join us. The three of us kneel on the hard floor and close our eyes.

"Dear Father, our Christ. I beg you to keep vigil over us all this night. I freely confess my sins, of which there are many…"

As I stop speaking, there is suddenly a flash of light from

outside, brightening the room as if it were day.

"Oh my goodness, what is that?" exclaimed Seton, as we all three go to the window and look to the sky. There is a flash of whitening light streaking across the sky, with flames of yellow at its tail. "It's a portent from heaven my lady. Your prayers have been answered."

I smile. Was it God in his good grace replying to my confessions? If it was, my heart is now still, and I do not feat the axe on the morrow. I suddenly feel very content.

"Look! Down there!" Willie shouts, laughing. I'm so surprised by his sudden change of mood that I don't quite understand what he is referring to, then I look into the courtyard and I laugh out loud too. The guards are running around like mice being chased by a hungry cat, as two balls of fire, no bigger than a tennis-ball, have fallen into the courtyard and caught alight the haystacks. They are frantically trying to put out the flames with small buckets of water drawn from the river. It is comical to watch, especially as one guard throws his bucket in the wrong direction and soaks another by accident. The swearing and harsh words are not for a maiden to hear, but it is an amusing episode. We watch for at least ten minutes until all of the flames have been extinguished, leaving a muddy mess with burnt hay scattered all over the floor. The light from above has now faded, and I wonder again if it truly is a portent and sign from heaven.

I now have new energy and my spirit has been lifted, so I immediately get to the task of writing my other letters. They are brief, to Archbishop Beaton, asking for his forgiveness, to Bishop Leslie, asking that he commands my will and to my other Maries, wishing them happiness in their lives.

None of them take long and then with the hour past midnight, I feel I should rest, so I lay on my bed, fully clothed.

"Would you that I undress you my lady?" asks Seton, who has retreated to the corner again to continue her needlework.

"I will not sleep my friend. After all, I will be sleeping long enough soon…and besides, I would not want to embarrass Willie here. I'm sure he would be affronted by the sight of a queen in her undergarments!" Willie turns a bright red and I'm pleased that he seems in better spirits. "No, I am resting and will arise soon ready to face my final dawn. Please both of you, stay near me. I do not wish my final night on earth to be spent alone."

I lie down and stare at the ceiling, listening as Seton and Willie make themselves comfortable. Seton lays down on her mattress at the foot of my bed, and Willie spreads out a velvet wrap from the closet and lies on the floor, ready to give into sleep. I won't give in to sleep this evening though. I listen to the crackle of the logs on the fire as the flames continue to give out the heat, and the sounds of the guards in the courtyard talking in muffled tones. I'm sure I can hear an owl in the distance crying, but it may be my imagination. The night is still, and the rain and wind have now but all gone, and the sound of my breathing becomes louder within myself. To think that within a few hours, this body of mine will no longer breath. My eyes will no longer look at even the most mundane things that we take for granted. I will no longer taste the sweet deserts of milk and raisins that I so love, or drink of the wine that has soothed me often in recent years. I have not danced or played the lute for so long now, that I fear I have forgotten how, yet it is of no importance, but to do that just one more time? To hear Riccio with his beautiful voice singing a sonnet, or Francois giggling as he hides in one of our many games. To feel Darnley next to me in those very brief moments when I loved him, or the sweet caress of my mother when I was a child. The feeling of the chase as my hair flies free as I gallop through the woods, or the gentle strolls in the gardens of the chateaux of France. All gone. I close my eyes.

Chapter Ten

It is only a matter of moments later, or at least what felt like a short time, that I am awoken by a loud banging on the door. I sit up disorientated and look to the foot of the bed where Seton was, yet she has gone. Willie is also absent too. I feel confused as I don't recall hearing either of them leave the room, and also, why would they? I asked them both to stay with me this evening, and they have both departed. An anger takes over me and I have to breathe calmly to remind myself that this is my last night on earth. I should not be angry. The banging starts again.

"Who is banging so loudly on my bedchamber door?" I say loudly.

"There is an extremely important visitor my lady. I pray you open the door immediately." It is Shrewsbury's voice, yet I was sure he had left the castle earlier this evening. "I think you will be happy to meet this person madam."

I sigh and immediately get off the bed, straightening my crumpled dress, and rearranging the ruff around my collar. My hair-wig is unruly, and I try to pin it up away from my face, but it is not like my own. It is unmanageable and feels more like cotton in my fingers. Whoever is visiting will have to take me for the way I am. I have long since abandoned any pretence of elegance, and especially on this night of all nights.

"Enter" I say softly, and await the important visitor, although I have little clue who it might be. Shrewsbury stands there, wearing a curious frock of grey that is embroidered with purple patterns, and a doublet and hose that I had not seen earlier. I momentarily thought it strange that he should have changed his clothing at the end of the day.

"My lady," and he bows to me again. "I had no idea this had been arranged...no-one had informed me...if I'd known I obviously would have warned you, but I am as much in the dark as you may be now..."

"Stop my earl!" I interrupt and put a hand up to halt his gibbering. He really is flushed and embarrassed by something. "Please stop, and just tell me who it is who is visiting me unannounced?"

"My lady, it's the queen..."

I stand there looking at him and wondering if he has temporarily taken leave of his senses. He obviously sees my confusion.

"What I mean my queen, is...well it's the queen. It's her Majesty. She is here..." He stands aside and allows my visitor to enter the room. At first, I have no recognition. I don't have an earthly idea who this is. I stare at this woman and she stares at me. She is quite tall with a shock of red hair hidden under a beaver hat. She is wearing a thick red mantle and is pulling off her white silk gloves. It's clear she has travelled as there are mud splashes on her riding-boots, and I see as she takes off her heavy coat and undoes her hat, that she is wearing an equally stunning red dress that shows her ample bosom and highlights the numerous beads around her neck. She stands there...regally.

"Mary...my cousin."

It is more than I can bare, and I sit back on the edge of my bed gasping for breath, I am so shocked. Could it be? Is it really? Now?

"Elizabeth...?"

She nods and then smiles, showing her teeth, which are not white like mine. "May I sit? I have travelled so many miles to see you."

I point to the table by the window and she takes the seat that Seton was sitting on just an hour or so ago.

"Will you at least join me Mary? It has been so long since we first agreed to meet, it would be unbecoming if we didn't at least face each other."

I am still almost speechless, but I gather my wits about me and sit opposite her. Shrewsbury quietly closes the door and I realise I am finally here, alone with Elizabeth, my sister, my cousin, my jailor, the Queen of England.

"I took the opportunity of ordering food and drink. I am famished after the ride, and a stomach of wine and pheasant is so welcoming now. I trust you will join me?"

I nod, but still the words can't and won't come out. Elizabeth sits there opposite me. She looks regal. She looks like the queen that she is, yet I feel I have diminished in her presence from the moment she stepped into the room. I feel old and haggard and ugly, yet she is not beautiful. There is a manly look to her face. Her mouth is small and her painted lips thin. The eyes dart constantly, and her nose is unpronounced. It's her hair that makes her desirable. Long red locks that have fallen over her shoulders, giving her an almost childlike-look. This is the queen I have heard so much about. This is the queen I have seen in miniatures. This is the queen I have desired to meet for so long. This is the queen who has had me imprisoned for over twenty years.

"It's not really fitting for a queen is it?" she says, looking around at my sparse chamber. "I'm sorry. I didn't realise. My courtiers hide most things from me I'm afraid. I didn't even know you were here in Fotheringhay until last December."

"Really…?" It's only the second thing I've said.

"No, I beg you to believe me. I thought that you were still in Sheffield. They had other plans though." The last sentence sounded like it was said in a conspiratorial tone, but surely that's my imagination. "When I heard that it was tomorrow, then I had to come and see you. It is time we talked Mary."

At that point a servant came into the room without knocking and placed on the table a huge flagon of wine and three plates full of pheasant, pigeon, steamed vegetables and sweetmeats. I haven't seen so much food for years. Elizabeth dismissed him, as he was not part of my retinue, and immediately decided to help herself.

"We can't talk on an empty-stomach though, can we?" and with that she proceeds to devour whatever food she can stab on her fork and push into her mouth. I pick at a few things and take a sip of wine, but I sit there in fascination as this queen feeds her more-than-healthy appetite. Eventually after picking the remnants of the poultry clean and taking a second helping of raisin bread, she is finished. I have not seen a lady with such a fondness for food, yet she is of a healthy nature. As if called by her in a whisper that I could not hear, the same servant returns and clears the table.

"Leave the wine. There is a-plenty to keep us company on this cold evening." She demands, and the servant boy bows and leaves us alone. "So, Mary, you must see me as a harsh mistress. Your tormentor even?" She leans forward on the table towards me and clasps her hands together, "Yet I have always loved you as my cousin. As we are of royal blood, surely you must see that?"

"I know my lady, that you have kept me imprisoned here in this damnable country for nigh on twenty-two years!" My tone surprises me, especially as these are the first real words I say to the woman whose company I have desired to be in more than any other. Elizabeth leans back on her chair and looks out of the window. Gradually she replies.

"Mary, you have coveted my title since you fled to France," her voice is almost melancholy. "Once you lost your husband and the regency of that country, you turned your attentions to me. I had no quarrel with you, yet you schemed and plotted to take my crown…all in the name of that abominable faith of yours and the backing of the pope too. Could you not see how wrong you were?"

I feel like I am being attacked already like a naughty schoolgirl, and the years of frustration at this woman's contempt for me start to bubble and ferment in my mind. "I fled to France when I was yet a six-year-old girl, no lover of independence from my dear mother, all because of your father. He wanted me and in turn Scotland. Can you imagine the tears that I shed or the loneliness that I felt?"

"Yet, you loved France. You were at home in their frippery of the court, their effeminate manners and their love of grandiose gestures. You belonged to France Mary, or should I say *Marie?* Why did you leave? Why return to Scotland? I refused you passage on the sea, yet still you returned."

"My husband was dead if you can but recall madam. My mother was dead, hounded by English soldiers, and my dear father-in-law also departed. France was no longer welcoming." I feel I have to defend myself, but from what? Is this how our meeting will be? After all this time, just accusations and suspicions?

"You could have stayed Mary. You had a dowry. You had the right to any chateau of your choosing. You could have married anyone who took your fancy, and I have been told of your legendary beauty…" I feel uncomfortable as she looks at me, seeing the lines around my eyes, the blotchy skin from too many years locked away inside and the badly-fitting wig of hair that I am forced to wear. "Yet, you forsook all of the pleasures of life to return to that barbarous country. What could have possessed you my cousin? What honeypot did the country have that attracted the queen bee? I have asked myself so many times, and yet I do not have the answer."

"I was…I am the queen." I reply.

"Ahh yes, the Catholic queen of a Protestant country. Never has a union been so stretched…Do you remember John Knox?" The question is completely unexpected and said in a mischievous manner. How does this lady change her moods and tone so quickly? Already I realise that she is far from what I had imagined. Her eyes dart hither and thither and her mind seems to work in the same way.

"Knox? Yes, I remember the odious man that he was. He made my life as difficult and unpleasant as if he was my enduring mortal enemy. Never has a man had such a feeling of hatred for me, of that I am sure."

"Really?" says Elizabeth, her eyebrows rising in disbelief.

"That's a far thing to say my sister…anyway, he wrote that ridiculous tome, the march of the trumpet against the monstrous regime of women, or some other incomprehensible title. It was about me you know. Oh, also about queen Catherine in France, you remember her of course, and I think he had your mother in mind too. He probably foresaw your arrival. He was right though…"

"What madam? Have you lost your mind? A sitting queen and you allow yourself to be seduced by the ramblings of this firebrand? I am truly shocked my Elizabeth."

"You call me your Elizabeth. That makes me happy Mary," she smiles radiantly, and I see how men can desire her, despite her masculine features. "I refer to his belief that England and Scotland have to be Protestant. There is no place here for papal heresy. You wear your beads around your neck and you take the Mass and make the sign of the cross, yet you insult and dishonour the people of your country. You cannot be queen and ignore your subjects. You have had no grace and you display no regency in your affairs. Your end was predicted, yet only you, as a foolish girl, could not see the path you were treading."

"I was an anointed queen and I had to return to finish my mother's work. I could not leave the kingdom in the hands of my brother…" I almost regret saying it, but it's is true now, even if not then.

"Such malcontent in one's own family. I have never heard the like," she sighed with a righteous air. "Ah, but a husband was what you needed, and I supplied him. It is to your shame madam that he was treated in such a dolorous way. A better match has never been found in all kingdom."

I look at her. I don't recognise the face. Despite the many

miniatures I have received where I believe I'd take note of her at a glance, this harsh and unforgiving visage is foreign to me. She is cruel, and her words are stern. This is the woman I put my hopes to, yet she never once embraced me or my life. I begin to wonder at the reason for her presence? Is it to taunt me in my final hours? Is it to exert some hold on my person, even though it is she who has signed my death warrant? I desired to meet her for so many years, yet now that she is here…

"You do realise Mary, that the moment news reached me of the terrible death that befell Darnley, that we could never be sisters? He was your king. He was your husband. I found it pleasing to my heart that you had taken him to yours, but it was all a deceit."

"He was not a noble man." I feel I have to fight back. This is nonsense and she has no understanding. "You sent him as you know what kind of a person he was. He was wild and ambitious and cruel and drunkard. He strutted around the court with ungainly ways, and he took mistresses under my nose, if not walking the streets and defiling himself with the whores of the night. He disgraced his standing, his family, his queen and he disgraced you, for it was you who desired our betrothal. He was a murderer!" I am angry now, and yet on this evening I should not be angry with anyone, not least the queen who has finally made the journey to see me. I take a deep breath and lower my voice.

"I regret my harsh words Elizabeth…" and I look down in shame, but she does not listen or chooses not to hear.

"You accused him of murder, yet your dalliances with that Italian hunchback sent him to the grave, whilst all the time denying your husband what was his right. Was it any fault of his that he should choose a course of action that would prove his betrayal by you?"

"I did not dally with Riccio!", I say loudly, still trying to keep my calm. "He was my trusted friend and I cherished him as such, and who are you to proclaim the rules of a marriage, when it is well-known throughout your kingdom that you have desired Robert Dudley in such a way that you turned a blind eye when his wife was removed? If there is a cloud on my character, then there is a stain on yours...!"

That seemed to work as I see her face blanch, and we sit in silence for a while, the only sound that of the raindrops that continually tap on the window pane. The fire is still glowing heartily, despite it not being tended to for a while. In the half-light, I see her face half-hidden in darkness, and there is a pain to it. I realise I have caught a nerve of her understanding. I feel guilty and ashamed, but why? Presently, she replies.

"I would never have married that ruffian though...after everything, the threats to your crown, the bloodshed in Holyrood, the terrible affair of Darnley, and despite all of this, you marry Bothwell. Are you of sound mind Mary? Is there an illness in your head that makes you behave so? I have made my mistakes, but my love for Dudley has never clouded my judgement or interfered with my ruling England. I am married to my country, yet you are married to whoever shows you his hand. How can Scotland prosper under such foolishness?"

She is right. I want to say to her that I was forced by Bothwell, but she would refuse to listen. Like me, she is a queen and a queen should rule, no matter what. My mistake has been not to govern strongly at times, of allowing my people to live their lives in a way that pleases them, yet it has been my downfall, of that I know I am guilty.

"I was maltreated" is all I can say. I feel tears welling in my eyes, but I refuse to allow them to appear. I will not allow Elizabeth to see them. Her opinion of me is lowly enough without her sympathy too. How can I tell her that Bothwell raped me? How can I tell her that he forced the marriage against my will? How?

"And your lords too!" she continued. "How many of them stood by you, then turned their backs, before reversing and promising their loyalty, before then vanishing again? Is that any way to rule a kingdom?"

"I cannot be blamed for the flimsiness of their characters. They had no more loyalty to me than a cat has to the one who forgets to feed it. I did my best, but I was always alone. There was no-one who would help and guide. I had nobody of authority who would stand by me do my bidding. Scotland is a traitorous country, and I had not the power to govern."

"Oh, spare me the whinnying! You were Queen of Scotland, but never has a country had a more indecisive ruler. Locking you away was the best thing I could have done. Anything else would have been criminal and only the Lord knows what havoc you would have wreaked if I'd allowed you to roam England unfettered!"

I am deeply shocked. These words are bitter and hurtful, and I cannot believe I am hearing them. Is this truly the way Elizabeth feels? No one has ever spoken this way to me before, except the hateful Catherine de Medici, yet here I am listening to my cousin, no longer a sister, talking to me is if I am a scullery girl.

"I came to England for your help…" I reply, almost in a whisper.

"You came to hide. There was no-one at your side if your memory recollects. Remember Carberry Hill? How many stood by you? Even your Bothwell deserted. That fine upstanding man, who promised on an oath that he would protect you, ran away as quickly as his horse would take him, only to a damp and squalid final resting place, not that his soul would rest easily. No madam, you came to England to save yourself, and I had no mind to follow your wishes."

"Yet you had me believe that my liberty would be given at a moment's notice?"

"I did not. That was your girlish and foolish mind. You had enough advice, but you heeded none. Even your decision to flee Scotland at the dawn of day was on a scale of idiocy. France called you, yet you closed your ears and heard the sweet song of England. That song wasn't sung Mary. We did not call you."

How could she know that? None of my courtiers have ever expressed those moments to anyone. They are loyal, and I know them. What kind of powerful spirit does she have? Does she read my mind? I feel lost as if I am summoned to the chambers of my uncles in France when I failed in a duty to them. I remember the scolding I received, and now this is of the same.

"Do you have no empathy in your heart madam for your cousin? A queen, like yourself, who throws herself at your mercy, and yet you do nothing but keep me in chains for so many years? What did I do to offend you so?"

"You do not offend me Mary, but your religion does. Your stupidity too…"

"You accuse me of murder and adultery, yet I could not have your conscience."

"You called yourself Queen of England when you were in France, even though I was on the throne. I cannot forget that."

"I was, and still am, the rightful heir. You know you are the bastard daughter…"

I sigh and close my eyes again. It has always been my failsafe in such times, as I can pretend and imagine that the world is not as I see it, but as I want it. All is still, and I care not for what Elizabeth is thinking now or doing. Finally opening them after a minute or so, I notice the same servant again stood at our side and he bares another flagon of wine. I did not hear him arrive.

"We shall drink Mary. There is no reason to arguing, not on this night," exclaims Elizabeth suddenly, and she pours out a large measure for us both. I fear I may be intoxicated if I take more, yet this sudden warming of her heart is welcome, so I raise my glass and we drink.

We sit in silence again, but I remember that this is a meeting I have wished for these last thirty years, so I cannot allow it to pass without discourse.

"What happened to Lord Bothwell…?"

"You do not know?"

Of course, I don't know, I thought annoyed. Why would I ask if I knew? I didn't say that to her though but just looked directly at her. She puts down her glass and stares straight at me.

"Your wonderful Bothwell, the man who could escape from any prison in the land, the man who could evade armies and face any challenger…the man who forced a queen to marry him apparently and then left her to face her own demons alone…well, he died in agony. It was that simple." With that she clasped her hands once more and sat back against her chair, seemingly without a care in the world.

"How my cousin? You owe me an explanation, even if you had little to do with his demise."

"Little? Pah Mary. I had naught to do with his demise. Really my lady, you do see treason and betrayal in every facet of your life don't you? Give me the Lord's strength…"

She composed herself and then continued, seemingly with a hint of glee in her voice.

"He was imprisoned by the King of Denmark in some place called Dragsholm. At first, they wanted to use him as a bargaining tool against your dear Scotland, but I suppose there was nothing they required, so he was forgotten. They put him in a dungeon in a castle and left him there. I was told…and remember I'm a queen so the gory details were probably left out…that there was no light and he was chained to a post where he could neither stand or sit, so he just paced for five years. He lost his mind eventually…so I'm told."

The words are said in such a matter-of-fact fashion that I again wondered if the heart and soul of this woman had been misplaced at some stage in her life. There is no compassion or understanding or sympathy. I think of Bothwell. Strong and reliable Bothwell. A man as hard as a rock, unmoveable and solid, and then I put to mind his ending. How could one die in that fashion? Does every person who touches the heart of Mary Stuart have to die in such terrible pain? It disturbs me, but then there is now little that does not affect me. My life. My misery.

"He was never released from the dungeon? He never saw daylight again?"

"No."

Again, I wonder how that can be, but there is little point in pursuing the explanation as it is clear that Elizabeth has no mind to continue. Bothwell died horribly, just like Francois and Darnley and Riccio and my dear King Henry. Only my mother was saved from suffering. Only she.

After a while of silence where I sense that Elizabeth is becoming bored and distracted, I ask.

"Why did you put me to trial, and why did you not allow me to defend myself? It was only fair and just."

"So many questions Mary. is this to be an inquisition?" She seems almost pleased to be occupied again. "I am not here to be probed and interrogated like a common criminal. Please remember that I am a queen, the Queen of this country and you are beholden to my rules." She says it more in jest than anger, and I sense another bout of mischief from her.

"You owe it to me to answer though."

Elizabeth takes another drink from the cup – oh how she can drink this lady! – and sighs and answers. "It was the casket letters of course. I heard of them and they were damning. Even you should know that?"

"Madam, they are but not genuine. They are a collection of love letters, yet they were not all penned by myself. It can take a mere glance to establish that the writing is different, and the style is foreign to me."

"Yet you have not seen them in their current form, so I am

confused as to how you can suggest their content? Is it because you actually did write them and hid the personality of each to deter the chase? If so, you are far cleverer lady than I could ever imagine."

"I know enough of them by now. They are constantly used against me. They are not mine, but mere forgeries to support a prosecution against me. I was never allowed to see them, as you have now admitted."

"Ah Mary," she is smiling again, ready to taunt me. "Let me see if I can remember some of the lines of the most condemning. Now, how did it go? Something like…"

'Excuse me if I write badly, as I am ill at ease, and yet happy to write to you when others are asleep, seeing that I cannot do what I desire, that is to lie between your arms, my dear life, whom I beseech God to preserve from all ill.'
Or that other one I memorised…

'I should never be weary in writing to you, yet I will end after kissing your hands. Burn this letter, for it is dangerous, neither is there anything well said in it, for I think of nothing but upon grief…'"

"Stop! Please madam, I beg you to stop! I did not write those words. They are the words…of another. Maybe Anna, Bothwell's betrothed, but I did not, and I could not write such things. Do not torment me so…" I feel angry again, despite myself, and I am sure now she is here with the express intention of goading me. How can she bring these things up now, at this time? I know I did not write those words. I am sure of it. I could not have written such things…I'm sure…

"They proved your guilt Mary, in my eyes and the eyes of others. You know it was to Bothwell, and the date was before your second husband had even left this world. They make you guilty of that sin. I could not release you after that..." she waved her hand dismissively as if I was an irritation. I take a long draught of wine and calm myself once more.

"Those are not my words and I did not write to any person with those feelings whilst my Darnley was still alive. Bothwell was not my lover. He was my husband, but not my lover..."

"Pray tell Mary, how is this so? You take a husband and you then deny he was your lover? Do you take me for the virgin fool that so many others believe? I am not completely barren of wisdom in these matters you know?"

I steady myself and look into her eyes.

"Bothwell took me by force...he raped me...I could not deny him then as my husband as the shame would be too great, in your eyes and in the eyes of all my detractors. He was my supporter in battle, as he was of my dear mother, but he took his chances with me and succeeded. His doings were rude, and I shudder at the thought of it now...", I say in barely an audible whisper.

I think she is shocked. I watch as her face, cleansed of its white foundation, turns back to that colour of its own accord. She sits back in her chair and reaches out for another gulp of wine, and I can see her hands are trembling slightly. Holding the cup in her hand, she stares out of the window and says nothing once more. I don't know what to do. I've confided in her and I didn't intend that intention, but now my cousin is aware of the truth of the matter.

"Mary..." she replies quietly. "You tell the truth, so swear you God?"

"I do, as he is my witness."

Again, she sits quietly for a minute, or maybe two, and then as if the force of a volcano has been unleashed in the room, she shouts at the top of her voice, "The blasted blaggard. If I could I would hang him from the neck and watch as his eyes bulged, and his tongue turned black. He raped a queen you say! I would watch gladly as each sword would quarter him and laugh in his pain. I would nail him to the walls of the Tower and watch as the buzzards pecked at him until they were satisfied, and even then, I would not have the satisfaction that they enjoy. I hope his death in that prison was of an excruciating longness that he would run himself through with a sword to ease his pain, if he was given the chance…and trust me madam, he would never err have the chance in my kingdom!"

I must admit to being quite taken aback at this explosion of anger and vitriol from Elizabeth, almost as if the deeds were done to her person. I want to say something, but words fail me. Instead I look at her face, now turned crimson, her nostrils flaring slightly and her eyes alight with passion. This is the Elizabeth that I have known in my heart and mind, and who is now in my presence.

"You did right in telling me Mary. No queen should be subject to such an indignity. Why, if my Robert had ever…even thought of such a thing…I would…I would, oh my I need another drink…"

I smile, and she catches me, and she smiles back. After a few seconds we start giggling and then that turns into fits of laughter together. I, we, have no idea what it is that amuses us so, but we cannot stop. I feel the water in my eyes and my chest heaving with hilarity as we laugh loudly enough to wake the rest of the castle. What must they all think, listening to two queens laughing like fisher's wives after a bawdy tale? I expect the servant boy to appear at the door to enquire what concerns us, but we are left alone…together. We are left to laugh raucously for no reason whatsoever. I laugh at the absurdity of my situation, knowing that in only a few hours I would have left this world, and yet here I am, laughing like I haven't for so many years…and with Elizabeth. The one person I hated more than any other, yet the one person I loved too. Who was it who said that they wished that one of us would be a man to arrange a perfect marriage? How true those words were. This lady, who has imprisoned me for so very long, is now sharing my final few hours with laughter. It takes all of my presence not to burst into tears with happiness, but the joy is welcome.

After a while we calm down, and of course she takes a drink of wine. Then she becomes serious once more. The laughter ends, and she looks at me sternly.

"And what of Norfolk Mary? Why did you plot and plan with him for my assassination? Why did you promise marriage to him if he would arrange an army to overthrow me? Did you believe you still had power in this world? You'd been imprisoned for three years, and yet you still thought you had your supporters. You thought that I'd agreed to the marriage? Were you really so foolish…?"

Chapter Eleven

The weather was so cold and icy that the passage from Bolton Castle to Tutbury took nearly four days. Some of the roads were virtually impassable, as the horses and the carriages slithered and slid over the snow that had quickly turned to sheet ice. Mary sat in her litter and shivered uncontrollably. She was wrapped in as many warm clothes as she could find, but still the iced-air seeped through to her bones, leaving her almost rigid with the cold. At least she was on the move though, which was more than could be said for poor Mary Livingstone, who was so ill with the effects of the weather, that she had to be left behind whilst she recovered. Was there ever a more miserable sight than that of the Queen of Scotland being transported through the white, snowy English countryside, shivering and alone?

She'd heard about Tutbury, of how it was completely unsuitable for the comforts of a queen, and how it was completely the opposite of Bolton, yet nothing could have prepared her for what awaited her that day. It seemed that Elizabeth had heard of how Mary was living in the luxury of the home of Scope and Knollys, her keepers, and had shown indignation with an immediate command to move her to a less comfortable apartment and further away from Scotland. Mary knew at that moment that would never be any acts of kindness from the woman she had thrown herself at just three years ago.

"Will this misery and persecution never end in my life?"

she had exclaimed in despair one evening whilst sat at the open window in Bolton, staring at the bleak countryside. It was to no-one in particular, but Seton had heard and had tried to comfort her lady.

"We will appeal to the queen once more and hope that she shows mercy and kindness. There can be no greater insult than to lock-up a fellow sovereign in these depleted circumstances," she replied staring round the room. If only the two of them had a crystal ball and could foretell the deprivations to come, perchance they would have accepted their happy lot with far more grace and fortune.

Mary peeked out from between the veils of the carriage and saw through the mist of the winter, Tutbury Castle rising to the sky in the distance. It was an impressive and impregnable fortress built on a sand-rock hill overlooking the rather unremarkable countryside. She immediately smelt a foul odour, and Knollys remarked that it was the smell from the distant marshes that made the air so putrid, but as it was winter-time, the aroma was not quite as bad as it could be. Her heart sank even further knowing that this was what she was being prepared for.

"We must face this with stoicism and courage," she said matter-of-factly to Seton, but deep inside she was terrified. Her health was suffering, and she felt the first effects of rheumatism in her joints, plus a light-headedness that afflicted her daily. Her physician had said that it was probably brought about by the lack of fresh air and decent food. Tutbury hardly seemed the type of place to recover.

"I believe that Bess is the stronger in the marriage, so I've been told. Maybe you can strike up a friendship with her my lady, and she can treat you kindly?" Seton was doing everything she could to keep Mary's spirits high, but she felt depressed herself. Years of serving the queen had put her own life in peril, and each new prison for her lady, was a new prison for her too. It was a depressing existence, but she knew she could not abandon her now at this time. Too many others already had.

"What of Shrewsbury? Is he amenable?" asked Mary.

"I understand he is a kind man, if not rather weak in the face of his wife. Maybe you will find him more to your taste?"

Mary blanched at the comment, but she'd known Seton all of her life, so didn't take offence.

"I will need to fall upon their mercy and kindness to withstand this smell. I fear I may be sick before I even arrive at the castle!"

Standing at the entrance to Tutbury were Bess and Shrewsbury, waiting to meet their new guest. He was a small and unremarkable man, dressed in his finery for the arrival of a queen, but he faded into nothingness alongside his overbearing wife. She was neither beautiful nor ugly but had a handsome face with a large buxom body, bearing testament to her three previous husbands and six children. Bess was a woman who got what she wanted in life, and that had brought about riches beyond the dreams of many, mostly by inheritances from her deceased husbands and by her love of business ventures. Her main passion was the building of a new mansion nearby, which she had called Chatsworth House, but as soon as she received the news that she was to host the Queen of Scotland, sent in a personal letter from her own Queen Elizabeth, everything was stopped. It was the ultimate honour and one which she was determined to succeed at.

"Where on earth will we house her?" Shrewsbury had asked. "Tutbury isn't fit for the horses, never mind a queen."

"She can stay in the two apartments in the tower. They are one above each other, so she has room to stretch, and there is a view of the countryside from her window. She'll be comfortable."

"In the tower? The rooms that overlook the privy with that abominable stench? Also, the view is of the marsh which is equally as noisome. You cannot be serious my dear!"

Bess looked at her husband. She loved him, with his eccentricities and his foibles, but she was in command. She knew how to manipulate him, and this was one of those many occasions.

"Our queen expressly referred to her unhappiness at the comfort that Mary was being kept in at Bolton. Her jailors are now one step away from the gallows it seems. We have been given her trust and so do you not think it correct that we should show the Scottish madam that she is in fact a prisoner here, and not our guest? Besides, I have already arranged the rooms to be cleared ready for her arrival."

Shrewsbury nodded in agreement, knowing that there was nothing he could do or say to alter the fact. Mary, the Queen of the Scottish Isles, would be kept in confinement and would more than likely hate every second of her stay here. He just hoped it would not be for long.

Mary shuddered as her train entered the castle grounds through the drawbridge and she saw the huge structure looming in front of her. It was worse than she could ever imagine. The walls were dirty and clearly in need of repair, with stones lying on the floor where they had fallen throughout the years. Even from that distance, she could see a hole in the roof, visible as a black mark against the white of the fallen snow. The battlements may as well have not existed, and if this had been a time of war, then Tutbury would not stand for long.

Shrewsbury and Bess welcomed her as she stepped out of her carriage, and she immediately noticed the difference between the two. He stood two steps behind his wife, which was unusual to say the least, and his wan smile was weak and apologetic, whereas she was overwhelming in her welcome, albeit in a distant and aloof way.

"You must be tired my lady after such a long journey, and with the cold too. I have prepared your chambers and I will order my cook to serve up food and refreshments, and then you can rest." It was Bess who bid her welcome.

"Thank-you madam. I am grateful to you and your husband for meeting me here on such an inhospitable day. My lord…" Mary addressed Shrewsbury deliberately, yet was again surprised at his silence. He just smiled.

'I see already who the leader is here' she thought. 'I must ensure I deal with Bess correctly, but make a friend of Shrewsbury as best I can if I am to survive,' but if Mary's spirits were temporarily lifted by that introduction, they sank deeper and lower than ever when she was faced with her accommodation. The rooms were virtually bare, save for a bed upstairs that was unfurnished, and a small table set against the window. Although there was a fireplace in both, neither were lit, and she felt the wind whistling through the badly-fitted window panes. If that wasn't bad enough, there was a smell, far worse than what had greeted her as she approached the castle. In fact, it was so horrendous that her feeling was one of revulsion and she felt a need to vomit.

"Pray tell, what is that unbearable stench?" she asked, holding her hands to her nostrils.

"Oh that?" answered Bess dismissively. "I hardly notice now. It's the privy. It's immediately below here, so best not to keep the windows open, especially on Saturday when it's emptied. You'll soon get used to it. I'll arrange for your food and ask one of my servants to bring up your bedding."

Bess left, and Mary and Seton were alone. "Oh, my lady, this is horrendous. This cannot be. How can you, we, live here? This stench is enough to knock out a camel at forty paces!"

"A camel? Seton, you do amuse me, but you are right, this is truly an offence to me. I do not know how we will bear this." She sat down on the stool next to the table and shivered.

"I will light the fires my lady. We can at least hope for some warmth for the evening."

Presently her meagre belongings were brought to the rooms, along with a bland but large meal for the two of them. Ale was served, and it made Mary feel slightly better, although the smell of the privy was all-pervading, and she seriously wondered as to how she would ever get used to it as Bess had stated. By the time of nightfall, the room had lost a little of its coldness as the fire in the hearth had warmed the air. Sadly, the castle was not built as Bolton where the walls had small tunnels built into them to allow the hot air to circulate and so keep the building warm on a cold day. Instead, the heat stayed in one place and the closer you stood to the stone wall, the colder it became. Both Mary and Seton had to huddle together next to the flames to warm their bodies. For that end, they slept together in the large bed that night, but still an involuntary shiver overcame one or both of them during the night, as the iciness spread over their bodies.

The next day there was a small piece of good news. Shrewsbury had arranged a few days earlier to have Mary's furnishings to be transported from Bolton Castle to Tutbury, unbeknown to his wife of course. They had arrived that morning at around ten o'clock and Mary clapped her hands in delight when she saw the familiar tapestries and paintings.

"At least they will cover the cracks in the wall, so we may be able to keep the wind from whistling around the room! Oh, and there's my painting of Blois…oh how I've missed gazing at that. It always makes me happier, as I can imagine I am still there with the sun shining and everyone having such a gay time. I miss those days…"

Once Mary and Seton had hung the tapestries, all in strategic places to keep out the wind, and laid the mats on the floor with new rushes strewn around, the two apartments started to look presentable.

"Not really a little Scotland as we had in Holyrood, but it's a start. Now Seton, we need to do something about that noisome smell. I fear I may be sick again…"

It was then that she collapsed on the floor. Her face was white, and her pupils dilated. Seton rushed to her, but there was no panic. She'd seen this before and was experienced in dealing with the queen's fainting fits. They'd been there since she was a child and were usually brought about through stress and anxiety. She remembered when she had lain on her bed at Jedburgh for days, seemingly close to death, following the madness of the journey to see Bothwell. They'd ridden for hours there and back in one day, some fifty-two miles, and then Mary had collapsed just like today. She recovered eventually, but only after the priests had prayed for her soul and the servants had prepared her burial, so this would be nothing new.

Mary lay in her bed for nearly six days though, unable to move due to her aching bones and weakness of spirit. She hardly ate or drank and didn't receive visitors, except for Shrewsbury.

"My lady. I apologise for the sparsity of your surroundings. It is not of my doing you understand, but the strict instructions of the queen. I will endeavour to make your stay here as hospitable and comfortable as I can." There was a glint in his eye as he talked, and even in her state of illness, Mary knew that she had captured this man just like all the rest. Now how will she bear this depravity of surroundings for much longer?

*

"That was the most loathsome prison you kept me in. It was not fit for the rats, yet you forced me to stay there for years, and no, I never became used to the smell."

"I was never made aware of such things, but you can be assured that had I been told, then I would have acted." Elizabeth is now shorn of her shawl, which she discarded as the heat of the fire took hold once more. Her shoulders are bare, and I notice the jewellery around her neck. It is shameless, with its fine beads and pearls, plus a ruby ring held by a chain of silver. I know it to be the eternity ring that Dudley had given her, yet she was never allowed to show in public.

'Yet you accuse me...'

"I did not act on any assassination plot Elizabeth. I was not aware, not at that time anyway. You guarded me so securely, that my knowledge of any world outside the walls of my prisons was nothing. If the sun had fallen from the sky, I would not have known unless Shrewsbury had taken the trouble to inform me."

"Shrewsbury...what a weak and ineffectual man he was. I'm surprised you took a fancy to him, especially as you have always surrounded yourself with strong men, except your first two husbands of course..."

It was another insult from Elizabeth, and I decide not to rise to the obvious bait.

"What is to become of me?" I am not weak, but I have a need for an answer. My execution is tomorrow, yet I wonder if Elizabeth is here for a reason?

"What type of question is that? You will be beheaded on the morrow. Do you think I can change that?"

I know now that she is a cruel and evil woman and queen. So many times I had heard of her bad-temper, of the way she treated those who displeased her. Her enemies were all around her, or so she thought, so that she became paranoid over every act, movement or saying, seeing people whispering in the corners of her court. She has had people arrested for such minor things, mostly if they had any sliver of sympathy for my cause, and in many of those cases, she put them to death. She had her sisters and her cousins imprisoned and her decisions were based on fancy as opposed to clear-mindedness. This wasn't a compassionate queen who cared for her people, as I do for mine, but this is a dispassionate queen, who cares for her position above all else. I recall the stories I'd heard about her treatment of Katherine her sister, a legitimate heir to the throne, although her claim was not as honest as mine. To have her imprisoned for months on end, as she was with child too, due to the paranoia of the queen, is as abhorrent as it is morally-wrong. I do not believe that Elizabeth understands such things though. Now she looks at me, with her thin lips in a cold smile, and I see into her heart and her soul. It is unkind.

"You are the queen. Your wish is everyone's command. As is mine in my kingdom."

"You mistrust your position Mary. Your kingdom is no more yours than it is the guard who stands outside these doors. Anyway, you were found guilty and you must serve the punishment."

"Ah!" I exclaim in exasperation. "Guilty! You mean of that showboat trial that I had to endure for two days in the room below…the room that will tomorrow see my end? That was no more of a trial than a witch-hunt. I have been hunted down like a witch and now condemned like a witch. You want me gone madam…"

"It was a trial and you were found guilty. I cannot interfere with that."

*

It was early. Mary was tired and cold. The weather outside was stormy and the wind had blown through the cracks in the glass pane all night. She'd covered herself with as many bedsheets as she could, yet each part of her that was open to the icy air in her chamber, became cold too. It had been a fight to remain comfortable, and despite pleading from Jane, the guards were under strict orders not to light the fire. She was in no state of health to face the lords and fight for her life.

"They are assembling downstairs Your Majesty." Jane was busy laying the breakfast of bread, cold meat, a pear and some ale, whilst Seton was dressing her queen.

"You should wear the black velvet gown with the white russet and taffeta. It shows your regal standing. White gloves too." Seton always knew how to make her queen look good. She'd dressed her nearly all of her life.

Mary shivered still. "At least there will be a fire in the hall. This cold is making my bones ache."

"A minor blessing, I believe. There! My lady is ready."

Mary turned to look at herself in the burnished-metal mirror and nodded with satisfaction. "Even now, you can make this old stone look like a ruby. You have surpassed yourself once more Seton."

"Mary…"

Between them, the three devoured the breakfast and then there was a bang on the door. It was two guards, sent to escort her downstairs to the hall and the court-room. One entered and bowed theatrically, gesturing to the open door for Mary to walk through. "My lady, you are to accompany me."

It was time.

She allowed herself to be escorted down the spiral staircase, supported on her right by Seton, who ensured that she would not trip and fall. The queen now suffered from severe arthritis and rheumatism, and any movement was slow and painful. Each step was taken carefully and deliberately as if they might be her last. Eventually though, they entered the hall through two large wooden doors that were swung open on their arrival. The scene that greeted them would disturb even the most stoic. On either side of the huge room – at least sixty feet long and twenty feet wide – there were rows of seats, tapered like a theatre, so the spectators and clergymen and lords and earls could get a better view. This was after all, just like the theatre and they had paid for their entertainment. At the far end of the vast space, stood a raised stage, and there sat twelve lords. The Lord Chancellor, a Lord Treasurer, three earls (including her beloved Shrewsbury and the hated Paulet), four judges and three crown representatives, few of whom she recognised. At the centre, and placed ahead of the gathering, was an empty chair, with the royal arms of England emblazoned on a cloth of state, hanging over it.

'Elizabeth's chair…yet she does not deign to give me her presence. Even now…'

Mary was taken to the centre of the room and forced to sit alone on a chair that was carried by one of the guards. It was hard and uncomfortable. Seton and Jane were ushered to the back of the hall, so Mary sat there unaccompanied, and now beginning another fight to save her name, her crown and her life.

"Do you have anything to say madam before we get to business?" It was one of the judges, and Mary realised that she had to strain to hear his voice. She remained seated and then said with as louder voice as she could summon;

"I am myself a queen, the daughter of a king, a stranger and the true kinswoman of the Queen of England. I came to England on my cousin's promise of assistance against my enemies and rebel subjects and was at once imprisoned. As an absolute Queen, I cannot submit to orders, nor can I submit to the laws of England, nor do I know or understand them as I have often asserted. I am alone, without counsel, or anyone to speak on my behalf. My papers and my notes have been taken from me, so that I am destitute of all aid, taken at a disadvantage. I came into this kingdom under promise of assistance, and aid, against my enemies and not as a subject, as I could prove to you had I my papers, instead of which I have been detained and imprisoned. I do not deny that I have earnestly wished for liberty and done my utmost to procure it for myself. In this I acted from a very natural wish. Can I be responsible for the criminal projects of a few desperate men, which they planned without my knowledge or participation?"

She immediately felt she'd said far too much and in fact had started to sound like she was rambling and was repeating herself, so she stopped and looked directly at the men ahead of her.

There was a murmur around the hall. Then the Lord Chancellor stood and read out the accusations against her. They were numerous. The most damning was the attempt of the persecution of Queen Elizabeth and the subversion of the realm of England and its faith. He referred to the Babington Plot of past, one of three that she had participated in, albeit from her prison. The plot was to have her forcibly released by her supporters and, with the aid of Catholic Spain, remove Elizabeth from the throne. This had come to light whilst she was under guard at Tutbury when Elizabeth's infamous spy Walsingham had set a trap for her, intercepting messages she had written and hidden in beer barrels for Anthony Babington, a young and smitten Catholic supporter. It was an easy trap and one that Mary had fallen into as if walking into a rabbit's snare. Her letters were read and replied to until eventually one of her correspondences had referred to an escape plot that she was dreaming about. It was all that was needed to charge her. She remembered the day well.

*

"I have arranged for you to take the air today your Majesty. We will saddle a horse and escape the confinement of this place." Paulet looked down at Mary with a glint in his eye. She was laying on her bed feeling rather more ill-of-health than normal, yet her spirits had been raised recently over the contents of the letters that were being smuggled to her. Could Babington and Norfolk really help set her free? Now this. Paulet, a man who had shown no shred of decency or compassion for her, suggesting they ride out into the countryside. It came completely at odds from his behaviour, yet she embraced the opportunity.

"I thank-you sir. I do not deny that this accommodation is far too dolorous to my health, so the chance to ride again in the clear, fresh air is one that I cannot refuse."

Mary arranged for Seton to dress them both for the adventure, giggling with childish enthusiasm at the prospect of leaving the castle, even for just one day.

"I don't understand why he is doing this my lady," said Seton as she pulled her velvet cape over her shoulders. "It's a surprise of that there is little doubt."

"Maybe he has a heart after all. I notice that his rheumatism is as bad as mine now. He can hardly stand. Have you noticed? Years of being my jailor has made him a prisoner of his body too. Could it be that he now sees sympathy instead of contempt?"

"Whatever the old fool thinks, then I don't care. I just care for the fresh air today. Come my lady, let's show the world that we are still alive and kicking!"

"Not so much of the kicking Seton. I fear I will not be able to ride the saddle like that of a man, but instead it will be a lady's demeanour on the horse. Still, we can chase!"

It was exhilarating to be on a horse and racing through the countryside again. It had been so very long since either Mary or Seton had felt the ecstasy of the wind sailing through their hair, or the breathless pants as the horse rode faster and faster across fields, streams and through gladed-woods. Somehow, and with the aid of Seton and a more-than-friendly guard, she had managed to straddle the horse and was now sat at ease galloping along, as if it had only been yesterday. She'd lost none of her old ability and for a few fleeting moments she was Mary the young girl, back in France, back with Francois. Even Paulet, who was never a particularly talented rider, struggled to keep pace and had to constantly urge his guards to stay with her.

Suddenly in the distance she espied a group of riders approaching. Her eyesight wasn't good anymore, so she struggled to make out the standard that was flown, but then she realised. She was being freed! All the promises made to her in the letters were being kept. They had promised that she would be released and here were her supporters riding towards her, ready to overthrow the handful of guards and set her free. She squealed in delight, much to the confusion of Seton. She looked at Paulet, who was catching her rapidly, and saw the look on his face. He knew! He had arranged it! Paulet, the man who had treated her so abominably, was now helping her escape...

As the riders approached, there seemed to be little activity from Paulet's guards. Shouldn't they at least be showing some concern? Even if this was planned, then it was worth, for appearances sake, an act of defiance, but no. All was quiet and then she saw. The standard that was held aloft was not of her own, but that of Elizabeth and the man at the head of the horsemen was none other than Sir Thomas George, an ambassador to the English Queen. He dismounted, and Mary noticed his fine apparel of serge trimmed with green velvet, an outfit she'd seen before when he'd encountered her at Bolton Castle so many years ago. He looked the same, yet inevitably his features were older and aged, but those piercing and cold eyes were till capable of boring into her soul. She shuddered. Immediately she knew that this was not to be the rescue that she'd dreamed of.

"Madam. I am sent by my most gracious Majesty, the Queen of England. She is rather surprised at your actions my lady. She feels it extremely strange that you should break the agreement that both made together not to bring harm to her or her estate. She is dispirited by your complicity in the conspiracy made by you against her, and has ordered me to escort you to Tixall, where you shall be kept under lock and key until your trial."

"You are ill-informed Sir George. I have not conspired at all against your sovereign. I will not follow you to Tixall." Mary was defiant, but one look at the horsemen and soldiers who had now surrounded her weakened her resolve.

"You do but have no choice madam. Please follow me."

George grabbed hold of the bridle of Mary's horse and guided it to one of the guards, who in turn tied their steeds together by the reins, so as to shackle Mary without any hope of escape. She turned to look for Seton but could see that she too was being held captive. Alongside was Paulet with an evil and self-satisfied grin on his face. At that moment Mary hated that man more than ever. The day that had started as warm and sunny, had now turned cold and deathly grey. There was now no hope at all of rescue for the Queen of Scotland and her Isles.

*

Mary sat there unmoved but did declare that she knew of no Babington except the pageboy in Shrewsbury's employ. It was her act of loyalty to him.

"Madam, if I may just veer away from your many accusations, I have to tell you that Babington confessed all to our chief spy. He named you, even though every one of his letters he had destroyed. He recounted everything."

Mary blanched. She did not know. "Under torture I assume?" she answered loudly.

"He was found guilty and executed some weeks ago. His body was there for all to see, so as to deter any other papist follower from indulging in the same."

Thankfully she was not made aware of his full and horrific execution, being hung, drawn and quartered whilst he was still alive and in full view of the public.

The Lord Chancellor continued and included the accusation that she illegally claimed the title of Queen of England whilst she was in France with the aid and blessing of the pope. When she countered that she was the true heir to the throne, the other lords on the bench shouted her down. 'You are guilty! Guilty! Treason! Guilty'.

Once the accusations had been read, which also included lesser charges such as speaking out against the queen and planning marriage to the Duke of Norfolk without the Queen's permission, the trial began. It was a farce. Unlike the other show trail in Westminster two decades ago when she was charged with her second husband's murder – another of which she was not allowed to attend – it was clear that a verdict would definitely be reached.

Each judge stood to taunt her with her supposed wrongdoings, shouting her down when she replied. Mary sat there alone and scared. She couldn't understand half of what they were saying, especially as she barely grasped the language of English and at times struggled to hear the words over the constant din of the spectators. Each new accusation was introduced in a different time chronology, so that she found it difficult to remember the actual events, and at no time was she allowed to speak for herself. She had no counsellors or advisors.

"I beg you please my lords, slow down and let me think," she pleaded, but her pleas fell on deaf ears. She looked at Shrewsbury in despair, but he averted his eyes. There was nothing he could do, and she took solace in the fact that he'd hardly said a word throughout the day. She heard the 'confessions' of her secretaries of Nau and Curle over her plans to overthrow Elizabeth, both of whom she had rewarded once they had left her employ. It stung of betrayal again, yet she wondered if they too were tortured?

The trial continued and after hours of constant shouting and screaming, she felt utterly exhausted. The Lord Chancellor, satisfied with the events, dismissed the court for the day, promising to resume in the morning. Mary was led back to her chambers and collapsed onto the bed, fully-clothed.

"I can't bear this anymore," she whispered to Seton, who was soothing her forehead with a cold towel. "I have no defence alongside me. I cannot understand what they say. They forget that I am a queen too. I have no right to be put in this position. I am a sovereign, like the one who judges me. It is unfair…"

"Tomorrow will be better…" replied Seton, although she too felt the despair of the situation. She could see her queen fading quickly before her and she knew not what to do.

The next morning saw the same. Mary sat in front of her accusers, yet there was a small but significant difference. She noticed how each and every one of them was wearing a riding-jacket and boots, as opposed to the vain finery of the day before.

'They have come to their verdict already,' she thought.

"Madam, the accusations against your name are numerous, but the last one is that you did invite, by your planning and plotting, the possible invasion of England's shores by the Spanish." The Lord Chancellor was standing with the book of documents in his hand. He looked uneasy and was darting his eyes around the room, and it was clear he was becoming impatient and wanted to get away as soon as he could. He had a wife and two children to attend to, and this trial was a waste of his and everybody's time.

"Your accusations continue to be ridiculous," replied Mary "and if I had a defence counsel, then I could prove that."

"Your defence is of no interest here. It's your guilt we

pursue!" someone shouted from the side of the room, and suddenly everyone fell into loud and raucous laughter. Mary reddened and felt angry, but she couldn't say anything above the din. She looked to where the remark had come from, amongst the many spectators who had paid handsomely to witness the trial of a queen, but all she could see were crowing and sneering faces, some pointing directly at her. It was insulting and offensive.

"Would it be that your womanly craft would entice us all to your bed madam? Would it be then that you would show us your innocence?"

The laughter grew louder. "Maybe once, but now I'm not so pleased with her beauty…!" came another cry. Mary felt her eyes sting and she desperately wanted to leave the room and fling herself down on to her bed and close her eyes and ears to the cruelty of the words. This is so unfair. She looked around her for support, but there was no-one. Even her aids were at the back of the hall, not allowed to stand by her side.

"Stop!" came a loud voice from the stage. It was Shrewsbury. For the first time in the two days, he stood up and spoke. "You will have respect. Even if you do not honour this woman as a queen, you should honour her as a lady…"

Slowly the laughing and the jibes receded, and the murmurs turned to whispers before falling silent. Mary nodded at the earl in thanks and smiled, which he returned. Then slowly, and in some pain, she rose from her chair and stood to face the assembled lords. She needed to hold onto the arm for support, but she was determined not to falter or cry in front of them.

"My lords," she spoke confidently and without a tremor in her voice. "I have withstood attacks from your persons for one and a half days now, with false accusations of my behaviour, wicked slights on my being and crude and vile remarks that would shame a scullery-girl, never mind an anointed queen." She looked towards the spectator area and noticed how nobody would look her in the eye. "In all this time I have never once been given the right of defence. I have not been called to speak on my behalf and any answer I have given you has been shouted down like a crazed bunch of alley-cats who have spied a tasty morsel to feast on."

The lords looked one to another and stayed silent.

"I have been denied a defence counsel, and I have been denied access to all of the accusing documents that you have all learned by heart for this day. Also, you have given your prosecution in a language that I can barely understand and have deliberately confused the dates and events, so that my mind has become a maelstrom of uncertainty. I hear now declare that I will play no further part in this masquerade. I will answer to only two. The first is to God, who knows of my weaknesses and faults, and I pray for his forgiveness, and the second is to your queen. I will only state my case to her person if she would deign to meet me, but I fear she will not. For that reason, my lords and gentlemen, I place my cause in the hands of God and may God keep me from having to do with you all again."

With that, she smiled to herself in relief, turned around and hobbled slowly out of the hall, aided by the strong and supporting arms of Seton and Jane. Behind her as she left, she could hear the audible whispers from the stage, but not a single one of the lords, earls and judges spoke out to halt her progress. It was over.

Later in the afternoon, Mary sat by her window and stared at the courtyard below. She watched as most of the twelve who had sat in judgement of her, mounted their horses and rode away. There was idle chatter between them, and occasionally she heard a laugh and saw a hearty slap of another's shoulders. One of them, the Lord Treasurer, sensing that her eyes were on his, lifted his head and looked at the window. He could see nothing though but the reflection of the river alongside as the sun was shining, but he knew Mary was there, silently accusing him. He doffed his cap to the invisible lady, knowing that he would probably never see her again. He then turned quickly and sped out of the courtyard without a backward glance. Mary watched as the drawbridge was closed, and the courtyard fell into darkness once more.

"Well Jane Kennedy, did I not tell you this would happen?" said Mary, turning from the window. "I knew they would never allow me to live. I was too great an obstacle to their religion."

*

"Why did you want me dead?" I look at Elizabeth and wonder at her determination to end my life. This woman, my sister, my cousin, the one I have loved all my life, yet she has been so cruel. I need the answer to my question.

"Mary..." her voice is soothing. "We are too close to think of a world that does not contain the other."

"What...?" I am stunned by her response. "You have ordered my execution though..." What is this? What is she saying?

"Not I my dear sister. It was a mistake. The order for your death was put in front of me by one of my courtiers, William Davison I think his name was. He was my secretary, but not now. I didn't even know what I was signing…I thought it was some decree to have the weather-vanes in the tower turned to the right at sundown, or something equally as preposterous, but it was the order for your death. Do you want to see it?"

"Oh Elizabeth. Oh, my goodness. My sister…" I couldn't think of anything else to say. Here was Elizabeth, sat opposite me with my death warrant in her hand, and telling me that it was a mistake. Are my ears hearing correctly? Is the wine playing tricks with my mind? I look at the scroll of paper. It looks real enough…I take it and read it.

"Oh, you don't need to read all of it," she said dismissively, waving her hand "it's all pretty dull, but the third paragraph is the real crux of it. Anyway, Davison is no more…"

I looked at her in horror.

"No, you silly madam. He's not dead, but he's no more my secretary. I've locked him in the tower. He can't get up to any mischief in there…"

What was happening? I took another large gulp of the wine to steady my nerves. Can this be? My eyes were stinging. I won't cry, but I want to cry for relief and happiness. Am I to be released from this after all I have suffered? I read…

'We do will, and by warrant hereby authorise you to repair to our castle in Fotheringhay, where the said Queen of Scots is in custody of our right trusty and faithful servant and councillor, Sir Amyas Paulet. Then taking her into your

charge, cause by your commandment execution to be done upon her person, in the presence of yourselves and the aforesaid Amyas Paulet, and of such other officers of justice as you shall command to attend upon you, and the same to be done in such manner and form, and at such a time and place, and by such persons, as you think by your discretion convenient...'

The bottom of the letter is signed 'Elizabeth R'. I'm in state of shock and let the document fall from my trembling hands on to the table. This is true? It cannot be? How many times have I had good fortune taken from my grasp at a time that was unnatural? How many times have I wished for the presence of good news, only to be haunted by the ill-nature of my fortitude? Can this really now be my salvation?

"Why?" I look at her in wonderment as if she has suddenly turned into an angel of mercy.

"It is my wish madam. We are both anointed queens and I cannot allow myself to preside over your death. I did wonder at first if I should pursue the action, but I heard that Moray was killed by a pistol in a street ..." She looks at me for a reaction as this is the first I have heard of such news, but my features refuse to betray my feelings for the man who called himself my brother, for in truth he was a tyrant and a viper. I do not mourn his departure. Elizabeth shrugs and continues.

"As he is removed, then James doth make a worldly king. He rules in your absence Mary and he's a fine young fellow. You should be proud of your blood son."

The words sting as it is now over twenty-two years since I saw his kind, sweet face. Now my little boy is but a grown man and a king at that. I feel as if the years have passed by in an instant.

"He talks of a union between our countries, and as I am of barren stock, then he will be the rightful heir to the throne of our united kingdom, as and when that time may come. It may please you Mary?"

I nod silently. As ever with my life, good fortune is accompanied by the slave of denial. A denial that says that everything has its price, and the price for my life is to be removed from court completely, yet I realise I do not care. I have long since abandoned my desire for the trappings of rule, and I am content to live my final days quietly. It seems now that my sister will allow my final days to extend far beyond what I had accepted.

"Thank-you my dear sister," and I kiss Elizabeth's hand. All pretence of regal equality, all memories of injustice, all desires of her crown are now but a fading vision. She has saved my life, and I will forever be in her debt. My gratitude is boundless, and I want to spring up and fling open the door to my chamber and exclaim my fortune loudly to the world. Elizabeth can see into my mind though.

"As a proviso for my generous gesture though, you will abide by my wishes. Are you clear?"

Again, I nod silently. I know that I will do whatever she wishes of me. I am free. I am unshackled. I am alive.

"You will naturally relinquish any hope you have had for my throne, for the throne of Scotland and for the eventual throne of the future kingdom. You will leave this place on the morrow, and you will remove yourself from England to wherever you feel welcome, but not to Spain. I will give you passport to leave, but I will not allow you to fall upon the mercy of Catholic Spain. You will not attempt to spread your faith upon my subjects, or those of Scotland, but if perchance you find yourself back in France, you will of course find a home for your papist beliefs."

I continue to listen. I am alive!

"Your removal will be...what is the expression...? cloak-and-dagger, and it will not be spread abroad. None of your supporters will know of these events until they are done, and if any of them attempt to return you, or any other Catholic pretender, to my throne, they will be dealt with harshly. It will be in your own good interest madam, to ensure that they are aware of my wishes, and of course yours. Once you have removed your person, and your courtiers who have stood by you, from England, there will be no return...ever. Are you clear madam?"

"I am clear Your Majesty."

"My final demand is this." She looks deep into my eyes and I see the light of fire. She has won. This is her victory. This is how it will end.

"You will issue a decree stating that your marriage to Earl James of Bothwell was a mistake. You will explain the reason why. I do not believe that the murder of your second husband will be made any the clearer by raking over his ashes, but the shame you felt at hiding the truth about Bothwell will be a shame you will have to burden yourself to. It will clear the name of my poor Darnley, and it will one day clear the name of Mary Stuart. These are my wishes, and these will be obeyed."

I sit there. I am rooted to my chair and I feel I will never be able to move again. My battle has been lost, completely and totally defeated, but in exchange I have my life. I should be joyous. I am joyous. I will see the sunset of another day and I will see the beauty of my beloved France once more. What will it matter if I am defamed and my name is sullied? Tomorrow I will be somewhere far from this prison. I will wake up at dawn and for the first time since I was at the head of my army in Carberry Hill, I will be a free woman. What trifles are my experiences? I have life.

"Elizabeth, my dear sister. You have given me the gift of life when I had succumbed to the leaving of it. I am forever in your debt. I do not understand how this has happened, and in a quiet moment in a quiet time, I may reflect and anger at my life, but that is a sweet thought that I may have the opportunity of such a thing. I thank-you with all my heart and with all my soul, and God be praised, you are of my kindred spirit."

Elizabeth smiles her thin smile and then fills up our flagons with wine again. "We should toast our good fortune, for mine is to be rid of the person who has bothered me so. I say that with kindness my Mary, for never has a queen had such a determined adversary. This will be our first and last meeting, and so I raise my glass to you. May our paths never cross again...!"

I stand and raise my glass, and then a hazy feeling overtakes me, and I stumble against the chair, holding on to it to steady myself.

"What ails you Mary?" but it is too late. Elizabeth sees me fall to the ground as the dizziness in my head turns everything to black.

*

"Mary...Mary...my lady..."

I hear the voice before I feel the gentle tugging on my sleeve and the hand on my shoulder.

"Mary. My lady, are you awake…?"

I slowly open my eyes as the hand on my shoulder now tries to shake me, slowly but firmly. It's all a haze and I can't quite distinguish the face looking down at me. Where am I? What has happened?

"It's time Your Majesty."

Time for what? I lie there and allow my eyes to become accustomed to the light. They feel bleary and I have to blink to clear them. I can now see Jane looking down at me, and it's her hand on my shoulder. What is she doing here?

"It's dawn my lady, and we have to be ready."

The words don't mean anything, and I feel confused. I close my eyes again, just so that I can clear my mind. Where am I? I quickly realise that I am lying on my bed and that it feels like it is morning, but what morning? What day? Elizabeth…!!

I jump up quickly, surprising Jane who stands away in shock. "Elizabeth…where is she?"

"What…?" comes the unhelpful response from Jane. I see that Seton is stood in the corner, next to the clothes chamber, and she is holding my black velvet dress ready to adorn me, but I'm already wearing it. I was wearing it with Elizabeth. I then look down at myself and see I am in my nightclothes.

"Where is she? She was here just a minute ago…and it's now light. What is happening?"

I feel completely confused and disorientated, so much so that a dizzy feeling suddenly develops, and I feel I'm going to fall back on to the bed. I notice Jane and Seton exchange glances and I'm not sure about anything. She was here, just a moment ago…

"I'll ask you again…where is Elizabeth?"

"My lady…" It's Seton who is moving towards me. "Elizabeth who?"

"Elizabeth who? Are you completely mad Seton? How many Elizabeths do you know?? Elizabeth my sister. Elizabeth my cousin. Elizabeth the Queen of England for pity's sake." I look at her as if she has just grown antlers in the centre of her forehead. Has she lost her mind?

"There is no Elizabeth here Mary. What is it you speak of?"

"Not here? I have just been drinking wine with her. We have been talking. She was sat there, on that very chair…" I say, pointing to the spot where the table and chairs are by the window. "We spoke for ages…and she pardoned me. Yes, she pardoned me. She said it was a mistake and I am not to be executed tomorrow. Surely you know this? Surely by all that is good in this world, she has informed everyone as she left?"

"There is no Elizabeth here my lady. I do not understand what you are saying." Seton seemed to be afraid, or was it something else? Did she look upon me just then with a sense of pity? I sit down on the edge of the bed and calm myself.

"My dear Seton and my dear Jane. I have just had the most pleasant interview with the goodly Queen of England, and despite my convictions, I bowed to her role in our relationship, and I agreed to be pardoned. She informed that the execution will not take place and that the morrow will be like any other, except that I shall have the love of life again, and I shall see out my days in my beloved France...and you two will accompany me. Now pray tell...what is the thing that bothers you both?" I'm smiling sweetly, but I notice that neither of them is smiling back. In fact, they both look concerned. I don't want their concern. I want their happiness.

"Mary..." Seton comes to me and holds my hands. She looks nervous and again exchanges a glance with Jane.

"Oh please Seton. Out with it!"

"Mary...you have had a dream. There is no Elizabeth. The queen has not burdened us with her presence and as far as is known, she is still at Richmond in her chambers. They say she has welcomed Robert Dudley back into her favour...but she is not here. I'm sorry Your Majesty..."

I look at her and then at Jane, before looking back at her again. Both have pained expressions. I feel totally confused and I try to recollect the conversation with Elizabeth.

"But we sat here in the dark and drank wine. She told me that she didn't realise what she had signed, and she'd put Davison in the tower...she said I wouldn't be executed tomorrow..."

"It's the morning my lady. You have been asleep..."

"What...??" I look around, and yes, it is daylight. Where did the night go? Is this some kind of magical trick? Have I eaten something that ails me and plays my mind so?

"My dear Mary..." Seton holds my hands even firmer. "You felt drowsy, and although you insisted that you needed no sleep, you could not help but fall into a repose. We let you sleep, as it seemed the kindest thing to do. We changed your day clothes to night and still you didn't awake. I'm sorry if we did you wrong..." and she lowers her eyes to the floor in submission.

I don't know what to say. I don't know what to do. I sit there in silence. Did I dream it? Was it just the fantasy of my mind whilst my body rested? I saw Elizabeth though. She was real. She was as real as Jane and Seton who are standing afore me, both looking like they will soon burst into tears. I held the paper with my execution order written on it. Where is that? I felt the texture of the fabric, saw the black ink words, drank the sweet wine and I felt her presence. She was here. I know she was here…!

"She was not Mary," says Seton as if she can read my mind. "You dreamt it. Your face was twitching through the night and you were murmuring, but I…we, felt it best to leave you undisturbed. You said you wanted a clear mind for this morning. I am so very sorry my dear, dear Mary." She is crying now, and I realise that it was just a dream. Just a silly dream. Elizabeth was not here in my presence. How could she have been? There had been no announcements of her arrival. There was no suggestion of frenzied activity outside my chambers as the Queen of England climbed the stone staircase to my room. There were no guards in the courtyard. She was alone, save for the strange young boy who acted as a servant…and didn't that boy seem familiar? Was he not a boy with the face of young James? Did he inhabit my dream? I shake my head and it is now all clear.

I feel crushed. Completely desolate. Can life be any more cruel? After all that I have suffered and all that has become of me and everyone who surrounds me, was this the final act of torment? To have hope suddenly thrust on me and then taken away is the working of a wicked and vile world. I look around me, and yes, it is morning. I am in my nightclothes, which Seton and Jane have put on me whilst I slept, and the table is empty. There are no flagons of wine and there is no signed paper that details my execution. It was all in my mind. At this moment, I feel like I want to be sick, but I know I now have to face the truth. There is no pardon, and I will soon be executed. I will leave this world as I knew last night and the night before. Only my madness of mind has allowed those other thoughts to manifest themselves. Then I realise...

"What is the time?"

"It is a little after dawn my lady. A quarter past the hour of six."

Less than two hours! In two hours I will face my death. I look out of the window, and the winter night is still holding against the onset of the day, so that the sky is a royal blue. It seems appropriate. This will be the last time I do this. I take a breath and try to put Elizabeth out of my mind. She cannot torment me any further.

"We have little time then." I try to stay calm so as not upset my two dear friends any further. "You will dress me, and we will then have breakfast. Then we will pray together before I bid you farewell. By the hour of nine, I will be gone, but of a memory for those who choose to keep me in their hearts. Seton, please do not cry, nor you Jane. I will make a promise to Paulet that you will not cry, and then he will allow you to accompany me to the next life. I would like you both by my side."

Seton and Jane do their best at halting their tears and Seton then takes the black dress again.

"No. I will wear the crimson one that Balthazar made for me all those years ago. I think I still have the waist for it." I tried to remain calm in my speech, but I suddenly feel like I cannot control my breathing. I take a large breath and plead for my heartbeat to slow. I am still trying to contain the anger that is building up inside of me. How can I dream such things? Why was I allowed to sleep? Do I have not such precious few moments left on this world to sleep?

Seton brings the velvet crimson dress and I know it is the right thing to wear. It has a satin bodice and white sleeves, and the cut is of such that my neck is bare. I find that almost amusing.

"Your finest wig too Mary," and Jane places it on my near-bald head. I suddenly realise that in my dream I was the beautiful Mary that so many men had wished for, and not this old and decrepit figure who cannot stand to look in a mirror. It was a final reminder. She then puts a white cap on my head, so gently and arranges the wig to flow down my back. The days when I had such fine hair in my youth…

"My rosary beads?" and Seton picks them from the cabinet and I attach them to my waist. I am ready. Then Jane places a jewelled cross over my head so that it hangs around my neck. I have never seen it before, and I wonder as to where she acquired it, but her face shows her happiness in giving it to me, so I decide not to ask.

"When I am gone…immediately after," I look at them both. "Please arrange my skirts so that I am dignified in death. No queen and no lady should be disarranged, and I trust you both to attend to that part of my body." They both nod silently.

"We shall now eat a hearty breakfast, just us three…" and I sit at the table whilst Jane and Seton call to the guards outside to deliver the food. It arrives quickly, and I am relieved that it is a far better feast than that we have been used to for so long. They deserve to eat well on this our last meal together.

The plates are delivered, and the cuisine is exceptional. There is roast pheasant, pigeon and duck. There are numerous plates of steamed vegetables with freshly-baked bread that smells of a summer's day. Sweetmeats have been provided, and the delightful apple-pie that I had a taste for when I was younger, is now sat steaming on the final plate set before us. A large tankard of ale is supplied as well as some wine, and I do believe there is even a small bowl of water. It is so long since I drank clear water, that I'm ashamed to say I emptied it without a thought to my companions. It is a true feast. It is a final feast. My last meal.

Chapter Twelve

There is a bang on the door. It's loud and without ceremony. It can only be one person. Jane and Seton both look at me, and we know it is time. Our meal has taken over an hour, and in the pleasure of the feast, the time has passed me by, although how I was able to make that possible on this day, perplexes me.

"Your Majesty." It is the unmistakeable voice of Paulet. Here to take me to my doom. Who else would relish such an occasion? "It is time." He speaks loudly and so I believe that everyone in the castle will hear. My heart quickens, and my breathing is frantic. Don't fail now, I say to myself. Now, please don't fail.

The door is opened and there stands Paulet and a guard. He is striking in his black doublet and hose with a huge cape tossed around his shoulders. On his head stand a fine pointed hat of purple velvet with an ostrich feather of rainbow colours attached. His face, always stern, is failing in any emotion. "My lady. Your time is due."

I suddenly feel faint. No, this can't be it. I have things to do. I cannot say goodbye. There are people I haven't spoken to or written to. I promised to pray with Jane and Seton, but the time has eluded me. Just give me a little more time…

Paulet enters the room and Janet and Seton stand before me, almost in an act of defiance. He smirks and pushes past them. I see that Seton has started to cry.

"It cannot be now. We have only just finished our breakfast." I feel like I am pleading, but there has to be more time.

"It is eight o'clock Your Majesty. You knew this was the time."

I want to stop time. I want to stop this happening. I have prepared for this for so long, but now…No this cannot be. Seton is crying, and Jane is staring at me. I calm myself.

"My lord…" but I still tremble. "I ask of you one favour in my last hour."

He stops and looks at me but says nothing.

"If I give you my word of honour that there will be no tears at my execution, will you please allow my dear friends to accompany me to the alter?"

Paulet stands, and stares and it is clear that he is thinking it through, and then suddenly says yes. It is a kindness and I'm grateful to him, even if I am surprised by his leniency at this late moment.

"Don't shed tears for me. J'ai promis pour vous." I say to them both looking into both of their faces.

Seton wipes her tears with her hand and tries to smile. Jane looks a ghostly white. I feel my throat dry and I suddenly feel weak and I am trembling even more. My legs are shaking, and Paulet obviously sees this and says to my maids. "Support her as she walks. She is clearly in a fragile state."

I stand there and cannot move. In my inner panic I look around and realise that I will never see these things again. My bed, which has followed me throughout the years and occupied the space of each prison room. I will never lie in it again. My dresses that are hung in the corner in the clothes chamber, all glittery and colourful, yet I will never wear them again. My bible, which I now clutch to my bosom, I will never open its pages another time, and my two dear friends who have stayed in each and every prison, Jane and Seton. I will never see them again…in this life at least. I will not cry. Not now. I will not cry.

Jane and Seton position themselves on either side of me and I feel their hands on my arms and gently guide me to the door. I am shaking. It's now uncontrollable. I fear that Paulet can see me, but in an act of contrition, he lowers his eyes as I stumble past him. I feel the blood drain from my face and I am desperate to drink something to ease my parched throat. Oh, my God, please preserve me. Oh, my dear Lord, please give me the strength. Oh, sweet Jesus, please save me.

Suddenly we are at the top of the spiral staircase and the room has been left behind. I try not to think that it is the last time I will see it, but I want to cry out that I've forgotten something, and if I could just have another moment to return and then I could delay the inevitable. I don't though. I shake so badly that I feel Seton hold my right arm even stronger to steady me.

"It's alright Mary. We are here." Her voice is weak and hoarse as if she has been sobbing uncontrollably, but I can't turn to face her. I cannot see my dear friend in so much pain, all because of me. The gloominess of the stairs is overwhelming me, and I want to run free. I want to shake myself from this and run into the meadows and feel the long grass under my bare feet. I want to jump on to a strong horse and ride as swift as an arrow through the forest, screaming with joy as we hurdle each fence and stream. I want to lie in the arms of my love and feel his sweet and tender caress and I want to kneel before God and bless him for my life and plead with him for my sins. There are so many things I want to do. I can do none of them.

One by one we descend the steps, each one feeling like the death sentence that awaits. It is the walk of the condemned. How many others has Elizabeth ordered to experience this? Where is her shame? Where is she at this day? Does she think of me? Is she laying with Dudley and giggling together as I meet my death, or is she in some darkened room silently suffering for her sister? I will never know.

Behind me I can sense Paulet and the guard, both patiently following. It is only now that my nemesis, the man who has delighted in my incarceration, is showing even a little humility. I say a silent prayer for his soul, even though I am in terror. Inside I am screaming in fright. I want to run away. Please don't do this. I don't deserve this...

Suddenly at the foot of the stairs I see my chaplain, Father de Preau. He is stood before the two wooden doors that lead into the hall, the very one where I was unjustly tried but a few months ago. Now it is ready for my beheading. He is in black and holds a crucifix in his hands.

"You will not be allowed into the chamber my lord. I have made that clear," says Paulet loudly behind me. "No papist nonsense here. We will observe the true faith in this building. The Protestant faith."

My Father bows graciously. "I am here for my child's sake. I will take but just a moment of your time to give her a proper blessing before she joins our God in Heaven." His words are strong and said with authority, so much so that I hear Paulet snort in exasperation. "My child..."

Father de Preau takes hold of my shaking and trembling hands and he looks into my eyes. I feel faint and I want to just collapse and lie on the stone floor forever, and never move. "God is with you. He is watching over you now my dear Mary. Be strong and be brave. I bless you by all the Saints and by God himself," and he marks my forehead with the sign of the cross. "Go in peace my child."

The doors are swung open and there are hundreds of faces now turned towards me. I freeze, and I don't want to go in. I want to turn and run as fast as my poor old legs will take me. I look round desperately to see a friendly look or gesture, but all I see is curiosity or contempt or amusement. These people are here to see an anointed queen executed, something to regale their friends in the alehouse or the gossip-mongers who will likely as not tell and retell the story for their own excitement. I am now alone, so completely alone, even though I still feel the presence of Jane and Seton alongside me. In the middle of the room there is the scaffold. I'd heard it being erected yesterday morning, but I am amazed at its size. It looks huge, with a wooden block at its centre. All of this, just for me...

I take each step towards the alter unsteadily, guided gently by my dear friends. They are quiet, and I am grateful that they are holding back their tears, yet I don't want them to witness this. I want to say something, but now my throat is so dry that I know I can't speak. I remember that I wanted to look to the sky this morning and watch the clouds pass by, but I somehow forgot. I wanted to open my window and breathe in the clear fresh air, but again I didn't. Why? Now I can't. Now I can't do anything.

As I reach the wooden structure the murmuring around

me stops and suddenly there is silence. There is a tension in the air, as if the final act of a dramatic play is just about to start, and of course that's what this is. My life has been a drama and now its final act is being played to the spectators. It is but a cruel play and the writer thereof is a vicious and unfeeling brute. I do not deserve to have a starring part in it.

I notice that my vision is blurred and only then do I realise that my tears are falling. Don't cry! You promised not to cry!

There is Shrewsbury. He stands alongside the wooden alter and his face is a mask of grief and deep unhappiness. I try to smile but it won't come. Instead I look at him and I know he sees terror in my eyes. He shakes his head as if to ask how this is happening, and I wish I could go to him now and hold his hand. Behind I hear a commotion and then the words "Long live my dear Queen" and know that it is George. I cannot turn to look as Paulet is now stood behind me with his hands on my shoulders, but I can tell by the noise that dear George is being hurried out of the room, his shouts towards me echoing as the door is closed. I want to rush to George and kiss him. Kiss him a thousand times and tell him how much he has meant to me. I hope he knows.

"Madam, I beg your forgiveness."

I look up and it's the executioner, his bare torso swathed in sweat and his black mask making me even more frightened. His axe is by his side, and only now do I really, really understand...

"I forgive you for all you have done and for what you are about to do. Please spare me any pain, more so that my friends will not suffer, for I believe I am already left this world."

A blindfold is put over my eyes, and the unsteady hand struggles to tie the knot, so I hold it in place whilst it is finished. It seems a stupid thing to do, but I do it nonetheless. Oh God, please preserve me. Please give me strength.

I feel a hand on the back of my head and I know I am being guided down to the wooden block. I can feel the grain of the wood as I steady myself and the coldness of the floor hurts my knees. There is a smell of incense and it fills my senses. God is here. I know he is. Whatever my sins, he is here. He is ready to welcome me, and I feel my body relax and my breathing slow down. I feel sorry for Francois and my mother. I think of poor Riccio and my dear Darnley in the flush of his youth. I think of Bothwell with his strong arms and I remember the friends who have followed me, sometimes blindly, and I know I will meet them again. With one final surge of energy that I thought I had lost forever, I speak loudly.

"I pray for you all, and please be assured that everything I have done in my life was for Scotland and the realm. I am guilty of nothing that I have been judged for and this day will have its eternal shame on your queen. I depart this world a happier person, and I would have you believe that my faith and my God will always protect me. Farewell my friends. I bid you adieu. God bless you all."

It is silent and then I hear Paulet say the one word that will begin my end.

"Now"

I close my eyes…

Printed in Great Britain
by Amazon